Mind's Bodies

OTHER BOOKS BY BEREL LANG

Art and Inquiry
The Human Bestiary
Philosophy and the Art of Writing
Faces and Other Ironies of Writing and Reading
Act and Idea in the Nazi Genocide
The Anatomy of Philosophical Style: Literary Philosophy and the
    Philosophy of Literature
Writing and the Moral Self

✻✻✻✻✻✻✻✻✻✻✻✻✻✻✻✻✻✻✻✻✻

EDITED VOLUMES:
Marxism and Art: Writings in Aesthetics and Criticism
The Concept of Style
Philosophical Style: An Anthology about the Writing and Reading
    of Philosophy
Philosophy and the Holocaust
The Philosopher in the Community: Essays in Memory of
    Bertram Morris
The Death of Art
Writing and the Holocaust

MIND'S BODIES
Thought in the Act

Berel Lang

STATE UNIVERSITY OF NEW YORK PRESS

Cover painting: "Not to be Reproduced," by René Magritte,
with permission of the Museum Boymans-van Beuningen, Rotterdam

Published by
State University of New York Press

© 1995 State University of New York

For information, address the State University of New York Press,
State University Plaza, Albany, NY 12246

Production by Bernadine Dawes
Marketing by Theresa Abad Swierzowski

Library of Congress Cataloging in Publication Data

Lang, Berel.
    Mind's bodies : thought in the act / Berel Lang.
      p. cm.
    ISBN 0-7914-2553-3 (hbk. : alk. paper). — ISBN 0-7914-2554-1
(pbk. : alk. paper)
      1. Theory (Philosophy) 2. Analysis (Philosophy) I. Title.
    B842.L36   1995
    191—dc20   94-48037
                                                            CIP

1 2 3 4 5 6 7 8 9 10

For Ariella and Jessica who
in likeness have
been two (or more) and
always in mind

INVENTORY

and PEOPLE

Articles of Incorporation

We have been used to think of writing as a physical act: the hand that pushes the pen pulls the writer. But that doctrine is clearly a fiction, at least from the viewpoint of writers themselves who insist that it is not the hand that does the writing, not even the arm or the shoulder to which the hand is attached, but some mysterious and common inhabitant of those bodily parts: singular, reflective, original (so far as they can tell).

But why—it seems necessary to ask—stop there, with this *one* writerly self? This question has special force for me, since I cannot avoid the sense that the pages written here are the work of not one but several authors. It is hardly an exaggeration, in fact, to speak of a corporation; and although the corporate name has not been announced publicly before this, the ring has a predictability about it: "Babel, Borges, Barthes, and Berel, Inc., Traders in New and Restored Ironies." As with any limited corporation, the liabilities of these partners can be no greater than their investments—one of only a few settings where writers dream with impunity of living beyond their means. (To be sure, they also have no guarantee of profits; for that, writers await the invention of the fictionless wheel.)

Why should this particular venture in trade have been transacted so persistently under the letter "B"? I do not know the answer to that question, but I would be surprised to find that the occurrence was simply an accident. The explanation may, in fact, be clearer to the reader of these pages—a possibility in no way diminished by my own failure to identify it. A text is, after all, much like a face; and if it is surely a favor of nature that the possessor of a face does not have constantly to be seeing it, the same favor means also that left alone to observe himself, he would never know that he had one. Arms, yes—legs, genitals, but not a face. And so with writing; for although an author may seem at times to be reading what he himself has written, he is not then observing it but writing it again, even when he apparently changes nothing. (Some authors are unable to restrain themselves even with the works of other writers; they rewrite these as well. This is another reminder that someone who writes need not also be able to read.)

To be sure, my partners, if confronted with the text I here associate with them, might deny or refuse membership in the corporation—and as a minority shareholder, I would be in no position to argue with them. But I would hope at least to soften that rejection by recalling to them what their own writings have insistently asserted: that the most honest and selfless statements do not create themselves; that minds without bodies have no greater chance at illumination or intelligence than do bodies without minds; that also in conversations to which it has not been invited, history typically manages to have the last word.

With ideas, we have convinced ourselves that we speak easily to (and through) minds—as we have also persuaded ourselves that we touch and feel only bodily. The most ardent critics of the mind-body dualism have failed to alter this traditional allocation or the Humpty-Dumpty Question attached to it: How, *ever*, to put the two together again? If change is to be effected here, it will evidently come only with thinking that is itself corporeal—through and through carnal—or, from the other side, as bodies are seen to move around each other with such discretion that only a hidden consciousness could explain it. That is (from both directions), as thought in the act.

Acknowledgments

Earlier versions of sections of this book appeared in the *Iowa Review*, *Michigan Quarterly Review*, *Soundings*, *Yale Review*, and in *Faces, and Other Ironies of Writing and Reading* (Hackett). Readings from the book—at the University at Albany, the University of Colorado, the University of Connecticut, Vassar College, and Wesleyan University—have suggested to me that reading aloud has a counterpart in *writing* aloud, and that this is how the pieces in this volume might best be understood (and, if possible, read).

Words,

One

🜚

"In the beginning was the Word" — a single word, we assume, and so the dream of every author thereafter has been to realize in his writing just the acuity and power of that one, only one, word. How else to explain the discovery of the idea of revision, of second and third drafts, the search for new connections and order — when the writer could more simply move on to other sentences, enlarging the present? Thus, he pares, makes transitions, evens the proportions among the fragments he first dispensed. Every change, every touch, draws the lines of the writing together, condenses them; the very idea of a line, constraining and directional, was itself an early recognition of this purpose. If the writer could persuade himself to keep on, if he had time and the patience to bear the silence of this labor, he would reach — a point. Exactly: one word that said all that he wished to say.

Think of the understanding a reader would require in order to grasp the meaning of that single word. In the end, this understanding must be no different from that of the writer: to read the one word demands the same accumulation of labor that had been needed to write it, the same energy, the same interest and impulse. The difference, then, between writer and reader would be accidental—perhaps no more than the difference in the rooms they occupy or in the light by which they work. Not, in any event, the difference between what they believed or what they thought. The claims of the reader of genius would thus be no less than those of the writer of genius: we might well insist that their names be printed together on the title page of the book that contained this extraordinary single word.

To be sure, even good writers may have bad readers. But that is another and less interesting story.

Clarity

We know that words can wound, and we often plot revenge by using this power of language as we nurse the bruises we have suffered. Let technology flourish, I say, continuing the search for a catalog of words to add to our supply of instruments. Some of this, of course, is already given: words that exhort; words, soft, turning away wrath; seductive, promissory words. With them all, however, a suspicion persists that these words, too, are no more than tokens. They seem always redeemable, exchangeable, liable to remission or forgiveness. They may thus be important not for what they say but because they say it: words as Muzak, white noise.

We need, then, a test: to see if there are also words for which equivocation is out of the question—where no remedy, no bargaining, no second thought, not even misunderstanding, is possible. The search here, of course, will not be comforting; we know beforehand, from the history of discovery, that such words would be difficult to find. But more than this, there is the menace of discovery itself—since we do not know how to handle the words safely if once we find them. Can we dare to speak them? to write them? Would there be danger in *thinking* them? The menace here is far from imaginary. For as there are words that wound and even with that are provisional, equivocal, countered by other words that heal or soothe — beyond them we would find words that, more simply, kill.

Reading

🐚

I asked my friend once why, with all the books, magazines, and newspapers in his house, he would spend so many free moments reading the telephone directory. It was a question, frankly, to which I had expected not an answer but a shrug, even perhaps a denial. Still, there it was: not only an answer but a theory. Numbered.

First (he began): It doesn't matter, for the telephone book, what page you open to. In this it is every bit as generous as the movies used to be. No myths attend it about organic form, about the natural place of beginnings, middles, ends. Start where you will, end when you have something else to do: what could be more reassuring, more reliable? But, second, on the other hand: there is also form and rigor. Entering blindly, at random, the reader knows immediately where he is, what has gone before, what will come after. And yet, thirdly: this knowledge is not cramped or fully determined; it is not without possibility or surprise. Free association itself could hardly be freer than in the reader who watches the progression of changes as one letter of the alphabet moves deliberately into another: at the beginning of names, in the middle of names, even at their ends. The streets provide geographical contrast—and then the numbers of house and telephone strike out in another, more enduring direction still. The differences of nation and accent gather in the names and places—a show of democracy marred only by the guile of unlisted numbers. Fourth: the rhythm of the book, its periodicity, within and without, is pleasing and not common. It outlasts newspapers and magazines, after all—a full year and even then, with the change, showing great self-control, a strong continuity. Thus it neither challenges the reader to rush along before it becomes obsolete nor overwhelms him in the way of volumes that test their readers by historical endurance.

And lastly, lastly: in a world where almost every written word is tainted, skewed by the touch of its author, who mingles intuitions, hopes, fears, in order to demonstrate the anxiety of his attention: Where else can one find so concentrated or consistent a measure of bare fact and truth? There comes a time in life, after all, when probity and candor mean much more than novelty or drama.

(Moreover—my friend concluded with parentheses— the telephone directory remains one of the very few books that I can read without the gnawing sense that it is I who should have written it).

Silences

Was it self-absorption or despair? We probably shall never know, for after a time the man who had once spoken openly and willingly stopped doing so; thus there was no occasion on which this question would readily come up. He was, his associates knew, quite busy: lectures, books, appointments. He had, as these accumulated, as his reputation grew, begun to talk more quickly, abruptly, always poised to move on to something else. Then his acquaintances began to notice him only move his lips silently when they waited for an answer to their questions (long before this they had given up expecting him to initiate conversations with them). And finally that stopped too, replaced by an intent and knowing look. It was clear that in such moments of silence no discourtesy was intended. For when a questioner asked him why he did not respond to a question that had been asked, he *would* respond, but in a raised voice, as if repeating what he had already said, with a note of impatience directed at the interlocutor who had failed to hear or grasp something that should have been clear.

It is faster, we know, more economical, to think than to speak; one might conjecture from this that, contrary to the usual histories, speaking preceded thinking. Like writing, thinking may have been added to speaking in order to extend its use (so when we criticize someone for not thinking before he speaks, perhaps it is not bad judgment or stupidity that provokes us, but only devotion to the past, a rehearsal of the species-memory). But what are we to make of the phenomenon of this man who believed he was speaking the words when he was only thinking the ideas? Did he, we might ask, believe that *everything* he thought was also spoken? For then instead of that character of privacy and silence of which he stood accused, the taciturn cover for which, with mingled respect and suspicion, he was known — on his own view of himself he would have been quite open and accessible, virtually transparent.

In Private

Alf and Beth were chatting one day about language, discussing how, at its beginnings, it might have been invented. It makes no sense, they agreed, to think of a language made up by only one speaker: how would he ever be able to check on anything? He would think, for example, that he was labeling a feeling with the same label (because it was the same feeling) that he had applied to it a time before—but what reason did he really have to believe this? After attaching the label for the first time (it needn't be very long after, either), there simply was no way of knowing that he remembered the "same" label correctly—since "sameness" itself would require labeling.

Alf and Beth were pleased to find themselves in agreement. They hadn't found much else in common recently and had each begun to wonder, in fact, what was happening to the other. "But wait"—Alf had a second thought—"we sit here talking about this idea, this argument, and we *think* we know that the name we give it—let's call it the Private Language Argument—applies just to the discussion we've been having, what we take to be its parts. Certainly, in remembering (names or whatever), two heads are probably better than one, but what if someone asks, 'How much better?' Twice as good might not be good enough (it certainly would not be enough if one wasn't very good at all). Couldn't we both, the two of us, be mistaken—just as either of us, alone, might have been? Let's go down the hall and talk to Gamble. He knows a lot about language; and he's good at settling arguments."

Walking, Talking

The mannerisms, the quirks, the stray parentheses of our teachers remain fixed in memory long after we have forgotten the pieces of evidence or marshaled lines of reason they urged on us when we sat before them, docile, complaisant, all ears. It is an odd requital, this. The scholar strains to bring together heart and head—his, ours; he offers to listeners an echo of labored hours, the extract of passion nursed against a cold of solitude, against the mild, indistinguishable edges of facts, against the temptation to submit to the disappointments of his own biography. And the theories unfold, elaborate, ornate, astride the full consciousness of a knowing self. So portraits are drawn of the metaphorical instinct of history, the genetic codings of art, the reproductive impulse of concepts and definitions. But his students, absorbed by that fluency, awed by the authority of an asceticism that punishes itself, wears itself away in order to add another world to the one given, nonetheless fix their attention on the gesture of a hand, the local rhythm of a voice, a necktie slightly, but always, undone.

The challenge for the teacher is thus clear: to give to words the contour of the body; to ask questions and then to shape answers as well-formed and definite as the bent posture

of a back, as telling as a stray piece of clothing. Few peda-
gogues succeed in these equations, and we soon guess the reason for that failure—in intention, not in ability. It is easy for
those who live by words to believe that the body is a contrivance of those words, not the other way round, that metaphors
shape the flesh rather than imitate it. Aristotle himself, the
master of those who know, could not reverse this order in our
thinking. Long after the immobility of death caught him, hold-
ing him to one place in the earth, we think of him still, first, as
the Peripatetic, the teacher who walked as he taught, whose
mind was so active that it seemed to grow feet. But here, too,
most of us recall this feature as a quirk, an accident of posture
or patience; thus we persist in keeping the body the captive of
the mind, its servant, even—at some points—its symptom.
Only a few obscure students, rarely heard, are willing to acknowledge their loss. These understand how much more they
would have been able to learn from the master—if only they
had the opportunity to watch, under the cloak of his words,
that extraordinary walk.

Aristotle himself, it seems, had an inkling of this rever-
sal. So he wrote: "The phrase 'in vain' is used when A, which
is done for the sake of B, does not result in B. For instance,
taking a walk is for the evacuation of the bowels; if this does
not follow after walking, we can say that we have walked 'in
vain'. . . ." We now, looking back, can only speculate about
Aristotle's digestion; but even so, we can be certain—as he
could not have foreseen—that he did not walk in vain.

Alone

There was once a man who prided himself on his sensitivity and his powers of empathy. He often boasted, in fact, that he not only could tell what his acquaintances and friends were feeling as he met them on the street or as he stood chatting with them, but more than this, that he felt their feelings, actually *felt* them. On a number of occasions he was even heard to say, with a half-laugh in his voice, that he often could not tell whose feelings he was feeling—his own, or those of the people he was with.

This was no smiling matter, I pointed out to him when he repeated this remark to me, the half-laugh still in his voice, in what turned out to be our last conversation. It might have something to do, I suggested, with the complaint he sometimes made that he did not enjoy solitude. Had he not said that when he was alone he felt quite empty?

The Realist

For reasons which I did not understand, I began, a few years ago, to walk in my sleep. The period of time that this went on did not last very long, and my walks never took me very far or caused me or anyone else much danger. Apparently I would get up from my bed rather quietly and deliberately, as if to avoid disturbing my wife (although it is, of course, from her that I learned about this), open the door of our bedroom, and walk downstairs, avoiding, as I do when awake, the one step in the flight that squeaks. Once downstairs, I would make two or three circuits—around the living room, the dining room, the kitchen, my study—without bumping into anything. It did not seem to my wife, who followed me on several of these excursions, that I was looking for something in particular; my route evidently was the same one each time, following the same order. She would have spoken to me or tried to awaken me if I walked around very long, but after going through the downstairs rooms a couple of times, I would walk upstairs again — again avoiding the step that squeaks—and get back into bed. The whole trip would take only six or seven minutes, and after she had followed me on this route a couple of times, my wife didn't bother getting out of bed when I started out.

As I say, the period during which this went on lasted only a month or so, and at most a few times a week during that period. Since I had frequently before this (and also since then) talked in my sleep—again, only for brief periods, but quite coherently, almost always, it seems, about the one of my books that I was writing at the time—my wife said jokingly, as we discussed the likely causes of the sleepwalking, that if I could put the walking and the talking together, it might not be easy for someone else to tell if I was asleep or awake at the time. My wife did not mean this possibility seriously, but the idea stayed with me nonetheless, and recently it took on a sense of urgency when a friend told me, quite by the way, about a genetic trait he had inherited from his father's side of the family. This trait seemed to have only one feature and no other consequences: even when these family members were asleep, their eyes would remain wide open.

I confess that when my friend told me about this, I found it hard to believe him, although I recognized also that this would be an unlikely story for him to make up. The medical books that I checked, although less dramatic than my friend had been, confirmed a pattern of cases of the sort he described. My friend was rather surprised at the sudden interest I took in his family history—but then of course, he did not know the background against which I discussed the matter. Since it is unlikely, no matter how hard I try, that I could myself *learn* how to sleep with my eyes open, I have begun to ask this friend about the occurrence of sleepwalking and sleep-talking on his father's side of the family. He has seemed a bit put off by these additional questions, and I know that I have to proceed delicately; he is thin-skinned and nobody's fool. But the possibilities are too intriguing to let pass. The serious question at stake here is how many people there may be who—deceptively, with their eyes wide open—may also be walking and talking in their sleep. To be sure, to answer that question presupposes that we can indeed identify these people, distinguishing them from all those others who also walk and talk with their eyes open:

those whom we ordinarily assume are awake. And *that* now turns out to be not so simple or straightforward a matter as we had thought.

Since Descartes first called attention to the problem, there has been difficulty enough in knowing that we are not dreaming the world we find ourselves in. And this was before we considered the possibility that the physical act of sleeping might be indistinguishable from the state of waking. Now we find also that the dreamer, walking and talking as he goes, may face the world he is dreaming with his eyes wide open. And what *then* would separate dreaming and waking?

English and the English

Is there a connection between sex and language? A bodily connection, I would guess, carnal from the beginning. What doesn't go into the one makes its way into the other: febrile, full of the promise that solidity will replace privation. I instance here the English—a single nation, but a complete hypothesis. Their flesh is in their words, and their sense of touch, it is easy to believe, is by ear.

Strike, if you can, a hot, sunny, and summer holiday afternoon, provinces or city. The parts back up, the waters take on passengers. What fills the eye, however, are not bodies but clothes—layers on layers: sleeves, trousers, blouses, neckties, overblouses, glimpses of apparatus underneath: chemise, undershirt. This is not, I believe, a matter of nature—the rarity of the sun, colder blood—but an impulse of character, even of principle. The layers are meant not to warm but to warn: there is nothing underneath but more layers. Where else— *why* else—do the women, girls, walk with, on top of the other layers, their arms wrapped across their chests? There is to be nothing that is *not* a layer.

Sex, behind a veil of suggestion and nuance, celebrates difference; it is itself a reward, we surmise, nature's sweet, for achieving distinction, for being different—male, female; one body from another. Further along this same line, the role of the orgasm. For without that conclusion, in the absence of a means of balance, of a *reason* to stop, the difference that first roused would go on to consume. Who could stay in one place, in one skin, if the temptation of difference remained always young, heated, itself cleft? So the orgasm—reason in heavy disguise—undoes difference, brings a pause to the temptation of another.

And so the anticipation of this solution by the English, their undoubling: the disappearance of the body, its denial, makes a reality out of appearance with its clothes and layers. There is nothing else, we are made to know, for anticipation to draw on, to hint at: that's *all* there is. So: now a presence stands—unmediated, precise, without ambiguity, no suspicion of another, no assignation for the eye, no obliqueness for the hand; great patience, a lingering on the present, direct, at once a steadying of memory and forestalling of the future, a form forming and showing itself.

But these are, we know, just the qualities and the will for assuring to language a great and imagined body. The effort required for this creation, I am confident, could only be voluntary, and it could only occur as the mirrored image of a passion that, without the mirror, would have been merely sexual.

Measure for Measure

No one who has ever been in need of it would argue that money is useless. But then, on the other hand, we need not have had much money to recognize that many things we would like to buy with it are quite outside its ken. We know the importance, for example, of having enough to eat and a place to live, or, when these are taken care of, of being able to acquire other, not necessarily large, things—books or records, a stamp album—that then become marks of identity. But think, on the other hand, of the many impulses we have and that we would willingly pay to have taken care of, sacrificing elsewhere if only an arrangement were possible—and yet always in vain. Would it not be worth a great deal, for example, if we could hire someone to do our worrying for us? Even for momentary concerns like being late for an appointment or the car running out of gas—and still more, of course, for those other, more insistent ones that seem inevitable and that we come to accept as natural: what the work we spend our waking hours on is worth, what our children are doing with their lives, what new turn the local or world politics is taking.

There are, of course, more banal instances that seem no less intractable. Most of us would be quite willing to pay someone else to exercise for us (so many others could do it more effectively); much the same would be true for praying. And then, too, surely we would be willing to spend large sums to have someone take over our headaches or to be overweight for us or to be a son or daughter to our parents instead of us. Even a part-time arrangement would be enticing here, affording a glimpse of life without the constancy that is now so familiar.

You will notice that I have said nothing so far about the most unremitting obtrusions that we would wish to buy our way out of: illness, the anguish of existence, death itself. These we would undoubtedly spend on to the point of impoverishment—and just such exigencies prove how slight the things are that money can buy in comparison to those it cannot approach. Prudence suggests that we should think of unavoidable debts not as debts at all, since we do nothing to incur them. But the fact that nature gives them to us for nothing does not prevent us from wanting to bargain them away: the problem is that we cannot find for them a currency of exchange. Even when we bring ourselves to make the most extravagant offers, we learn here too that in the end it is—literally—impossible to live beyond our means.

Order

Mystery stories themselves, like the innocent details in them that turn out to be clues, are not what they seem; the genre itself is a mystery. On the surface, it appeals to the reader by setting up a puzzle, posing a riddle. But does it expend time in this leisurely passage only in order to allow the reader to spend his? Recall what happens as the mystery is announced by the actions of an unnamed agent. The reader knows from this announcement that clues are to be found all around him: they are everywhere in the text—but disguised, under different descriptions, woven into a narrative of commonplace event and dialogue. So he must attend closely to that commonplace: it is not, or at least not only, what it seems. But the only way to discover this is to look carefully, to know what the seeming is. Even where ambiguity is finally dispelled, when what appears to be the case turns out *to be* the case, the reader knows this only through giving the appearance his full attention, by accepting it, by living in it.

And so mystery stories are remembered not for the puzzles they set or their solutions (the exceptions are recalled as exceptions: a purloined letter, a dog that didn't bark), but for the characters and worlds to which they give life, their portraits of detail: the eccentric resources of Sherlock Holmes; the hermetic sensibility of an English village punctured by the frail Miss Marple; the fat of Nero Wolfe, settled in his New York brownstone, sending his intelligence out to work for him on its feet. The mystery of the story, then, is at once a disguise and a clue, a nonliterary pretext for the literary disclosure of trustworthy and comforting worlds.

We should not ignore the fact that the mystery novel is only more open in this strategy than other literary forms. The classic allegiance of literary patriotism to an order—to beginnings, middles, ends; first the complication, then the denouement—has always been a ritual cover for the more simple pleasure that readers find in between those moments. It is understandable that we should make the mystery story pay for revealing this secret; so we call it a minor form.

Prayer

❦

Writers often claim that they write in order to tell stories, and their readers believe this as well. Moved or involved as they become, readers insist that it is the story that wins our allegiance, not the writer, still less the institution of writing itself: "Trust the tale, not the teller." I am uncertain why readers conceal the truth from themselves in this way, since it is hardly to their credit not to admit the obvious alternative: that the purpose of the writer is not to be found in the story but much more simply in coercing the reader, in *making* him read. What is at stake in the relation between writer and reader is, in fact, the renewal of a social contract. The writer on his side aspires to authority, granting the reader—in exchange for submission—civility, the offer of a community, an imagined life. Anyone who fears the state of nature, who distrusts self-assertion, will incline to this offer; thus, readers are born. And thus, also, to refuse this offer, to dare not to read, requires courage, a willfulness; it is a moral verdict, not an aesthetic judgment at all.

There is ample evidence for this theory of the origin of writing in the fact that for the reader, the particular words and sentences he accepts from the writer are often accidental (so, for example, by the time the reader decides whether he wants to read them, he already has); they are the surface appearance of an act that even for the reader continually embellishes its true motives and character. This concealment was shown to me only recently, as I stood at the entrance to the circular reading room of a great library. There, in a brief moment, I saw clearly what I had often, unseeing, looked at before: the posture of adoration and submission of the readers as they sit in their spherical rows—concise, restrained, devout. Silent always, heads bowed, looking neither right nor left, not often daring even to stand or to move about. I saw then, too, that this communal worship was in no way affected by evident differences in the texts over which they bent—something I had learned long before from the study of religious texts: the particular words scanned or uttered do not matter. Discordance, strangeness, even an alien language, may be more compelling than uniformity or familiarity. The writer's power, we understand, is over will, not over reason.

It may be too much to expect writers to forgo this temptation of conquest, even if we prove to them what their intentions are. Admittedly, those who write badly have the moral virtue of allowing conscience to show through; they at least try to warn the reader, to put him off. But even they, of course, choose to write badly rather than not to write at all.

Reading in Vain

I have passed the point where I am ashamed or even wary in admitting that I have not read a book whose title comes up in conversation, or that I am unacquainted with people or places whose names are mentioned. With so many things that I do not and to the end will not know, one item or twenty or even a hundred more can hardly make a difference for anything else that I do or am. So I have drawn the conclusion—it is not exactly an *ethical* decision—that I might as well be honest.

The dangers in this resolve for candor are evident. For if a confession of ignorance comes so readily to hand with no attending stigma, perhaps even with a reputation to be gained of forthrightness, then ignorance and not only its confession may be less culpable than it is usually judged. And even another moral may inch forward here, one not necessarily as defeatist as it sounds: that having managed this far and without shame to avoid knowing the many things that I have not yet learned, there is little reason why I should attempt to change this in the future, that is, to learn what more I might be able to. (An extreme version of this view argues that we may also be justified in forgetting what we already know, or at least that there is no reason for struggling to remember it.)

It is not without qualms that I face these conclusions and I confess that my commitment lacks assurance. Not from a fear of embarrassment, but because of a glimpse I had, along the way, of a contrary world. I refer here to the improbability of the Talmudic judgment that informs us that one of only a few occasions when lying is justified occurs when a person is asked by someone else if he has read a certain book. The person responding to the question, we learn, is justified in answering falsely (that is, in lying). He may—indeed there is a sense in which he *ought* to—deny that he has read the book although in fact he has. For the sake of modesty.

It is difficult to know here what is unlikelier for the imagination to conceive: a person to whom lies come so readily that this unexpected moral dispensation would hardly be needed—or a reverence so urgent that it builds a frame of humility and deference around books at the cost of sinning. In a contest of the book against the lie, then, the book wins; we know this because it provides, as nothing else does, a justification for lying. (All that it has to surmount after this, of course, is the steep incline of vanity.)

Signs,

Desire

The creators of advertising are willing to try to sell anything to anybody. They think of this willing suspension of disbelief as free enterprise, but the truth is that in professing this ideal they give themselves less credit than they deserve. To be sure, it may be that advertising does increase sales. But almost no one—maker, seller, consumer—is still interested in such claims. Merely assuming it so, the manufacturer prudently, reasonably, adds the cost of advertising to the cost of making his products. Thus, too, the relation of seller and advertiser is brotherly—the comfort for each of an allied presence.

What we have discovered beyond this, however, is that the buyer pays the seller's price for the advertising as much as for the object. This unexpected conclusion becomes more credible once we recall the human craving for language and community, the passion for expression that is one, perhaps the only, means of escaping solitude. Advertising, after all, adds words and images to objects that nature itself, mute and inexpressive, could never provide—that even the process of making leaves unformed and unheard. The advertiser, as he names, identifies, rhymes, sings, is in fact giving life: objects begin to speak in their own voices. What before had been dumb, indifferent to surrounding and viewer, is now filled with energy, self-affirming, responsive to human impulse and want (perhaps it sometimes mistakes them, but who of us does not make such errors?). Society is not only enlarged but thickened; we find expression on every side—in what we eat, in what we wear, in implements of sleeping or playing, in machines; everywhere voices sound, appearances reveal identities. It would be surprising—perhaps also a moral injustice—if the possibility of this live community should be challenged at a time when the insulations of privacy, of detached observation, increasingly divide us.

The final proof of what I am claiming here, admittedly, is still in the future, when someone with the spur of genius finds a way to sell advertisements without giving or asking any commitment to the objects they represent. This would not be the first time, we might then recall, that such a revolution had occurred: a strong precedent for it sounds in the evocations of love poetry. For there, too, the impulse for a tangible and live presence finds itself embodied in a voice—and there, too, it is the voice, not the presence or the person, that survives, and that later, even centuries afterward, stirs and maintains desire.

Gods

Imagine a standard supermarket, but with one unusual feature: all the items in it are sold for the same price. That single price is higher, obviously, than some of the goods would cost by themselves, but it is also lower than the cost of the others. No labels are attached to the individual items; only one large sign appears in the store, with the common, the one, price.

It turns out that the advantages of this policy are mainly political and moral—a seeming irrelevance which, however, makes explicit the truth we diligently hide from ourselves that economics is a branch of ethics (we could hardly expect the economists themselves to inform us of this connection). What, after all, would provide a surer ground for communal solidarity, for a sense of human affinity, than the awareness, whenever we buy something new, of establishing a strong common link with the other customers—perfect strangers—milling around the store? To be sure, this is to an extent true even now, as consumer demand evidently affects supply and cost— but we pretend otherwise, deriving a false sense of individuality, separateness, from the differences in prices or totals, in the possessions we accumulate and to which we then attach our identity. The commitment of this new supermarket would thus also strike a blow against hypocrisy.

There is no reason, admittedly, why this practice should hold only in one store. On moral grounds, in fact, if the policy is sound, it should be applied generally, avoiding charges of discrimination or special interest. And as it would then come to include all items for sale in a complex society—airline tickets, dental floss, mortgage payments—we can readily predict the status and authority of this one price that unites them all, the objects for sale and their purchasers as well. No person in the society could be unaware of what—almost who—it was: even children and illiterates would recognize the number as an icon. Virtually every action, certainly every decision of the community or family, would take account of it. There might well be songs written about this remarkable number, poems in celebration of its power, rituals associated with its observance, and myths about its origins. There might well be discovered proofs for the necessary existence of the number— since without it, what would the value of objects be? The very presence of the objects themselves would pale by comparison.

One can easily understand that as this new awareness took hold, people would be reluctant to see the price changed, not only upwards but downwards as well. Commitments that strike deeply are rare, after all—and money is not everything.

Catching a Fish

We think of pain as expressive, noisy, distorting. Some people are better at concealing it than others, but even then we believe that we can recognize the concealment. We should be aware, however, of the terrible mistake we may make with this confidence in the power of interpretation, in the reading of signs. We know, for instance, the tradition of artistic creation, according to which internal pain offers itself to the outer world as beauty. That example, admittedly, is superficial; often the beauty it claims is merely conventional, the result of habituation. Even at best, however, it is overstated, more than we need, since we can also imagine pain so great as to freeze or immobilize expression: agony in the register of silence. To be sure, we may see our way through this as well, to the lines or contortion of a face, the eyes rolled upward, and so on. But expectations like these may also be too full, too dramatic. What, more simply, if certain moments were so piercing—frozen by a thrust of the present strong enough to deter even the hope of change—that only the expression of normalcy itself remains?

We should hardly expect anything other than this, in fact, at a time when pain is final; that is, when it excises the possibility of all alternatives. And as this is so, surely we need to look again at the faces around us, those which we daily, normally, take for granted as unmasked, emotionless, calm.

Pointing

Philosophy has spent much of its wonder on intentions. The will, for Kant, is what ethical action is: consequences come and go, but none of them endures, none marks a sufficient stopping point. Intentions, on the other hand, what the person willed to do: these remain after the act, even, because of the breach they make in time itself, after the life of the agent.

It is just this idea of separation that has troubled the philosopher recently. Because if an intention is separate from its consequent action, it also ought to have a place, a moment of its own — and where, we ask, would that be? In the head? In the *mind?* At a secret point in the course of the action? Nothing visible answers.

There is a malady in which, some have claimed, we find the cure for such questions; like many cures, however, it seems to act slowly, requiring more than only the assent or conviction of the patient. The doctors recognize a distinctive motion that they name the "intention tremor." With this condition, a person normally with steady hands, not nervous or distraught in any apparent way, concentrates on a particular object, focuses on it, grasps or reaches for it, or only, perhaps, points at it: he *intends* it. Then the tremor appears.

We may well be inclined to say that for this person as he acts, his intention is there, in his hands: the tremor is unfailing as well as unmistakable. And surely hands do express designs and efforts more than any other appendage or aspect of the body, as much perhaps as the face, which remains, after all, however mobile its features, fixed always in one place. But if we incline in this direction, we have also to decide what shall be said for those people, the rest of us, in whom the tremor does not appear. Not, obviously, that we have no intentions — since with this, the field of innocence would be enlarged beyond conscience. One means of saving appearances would be to hold that the intention-tremor reflects openly what those of us without it have successfully learned to conceal. But that, too, would be to say what is already well known, and not only about intentions.

One by One

🔖

It is not an age for argument in behalf of moral principle. Criminality is redressed by making allowance for the criminal, his psychological past, his social present. Justice, too, presents itself in similar terms of displacement: tribal mores or rituals, taboos. And not only the strong moral qualities or defects are consequences of this kind. In an age of suspicion, even simple pleasures, mere happiness, require explanation: we admit no surface without an underside, no appearance without an unapparent center.

Who would think, then, that the traditional and unequivocal ideal of monogamy, of sexual fidelity, would find advancement in this same impulse for dispersion, translation, pluralism? But there it is, unmistakable, clearly shorn—a medical concept, now, part of the not very strong fortress against the insults of hypertension, the oversubtleties of heart disease. "What about sex?" the anxious recuperant asks. "Fine," the doctor replies patiently, "as long as it's not too exciting. Only with your wife (husband)."

Parents

When we harden ourselves, break the surface of appearances, we find ourselves face to face with biology—and so also in the case of parents. It takes years for children (that is, everybody) to see through childhood, those hazy years of wanting and growing, moving from suspicion to knowledge, the whole tinged with a presence that never wavers, that is close by even when harsh or estranged. The voices, the gestures, the rhythms, the commands—who can sort them out? Many children never do: the demands and the gifts are too severe. No child ever does it all.

But this sense of incompleteness also mirrors in consciousness the necessity of nature. For the main answer to its own puzzle is there, we recognize, in the question itself: someone must give creation a push and the wherewithal—and that, after all, is what we name as parent. This makes parenthood as well as birth a biological event, and few would quarrel with the justice of that claim. Yet this cannot be the whole of the matter—a lack we see quickly as we try to imagine the existence of people born without parents. Let us—their creators—not worry how this happens; we know only that they step into life healthy, active, intelligent. To assure their independence, let them be born not as babies but as adults (at most, after all, childhood is a convention), with language, with professions, with techniques for survival. The one thing they lack, that they have no means of looking back on or discovering, is a set of parents. They are not orphaned, not adopted; they simply do not have origins. And all we ask of them then is that they should go about the normal business of living.

As slight a request, it turns out, as to live and sport in the thin air of Everest. For what would we do if literally we had to make ourselves? Could a person spin himself of whole cloth? The evidence is all the other way. Orphans never, in the whole of their lives, accommodate to the loss, and children who discover the imposture of adoptive parents seek perpetually for a glimpse of biological reality. It matters little to them what brutality or misery stood at their beginnings—and why should it? They search not for kindness or generosity, not even for penitence—only for the evidence that they have antecedents. Only then could they escape the suspicion that refuses to quit: that having first created themselves, they must, through the rest of their lives, go on doing this, living only for and by themselves.

Invidiously, cruelly, intolerantly, we do not speak of adults whose parents die as orphans. This is partly because adults have lost the anticipation, the disarray of the child; they are too tired, fed too much by the demands of self to feel the absence of others exactly as their own. But more important, they have memory, the recollection of origins which, although as memory loses its edge has no surer grip on reality than that of a myth, nonetheless supports them in their age.

Sartre, that courageous figure of the intellect and spirit, gave a new sense to the act of freedom and the life of the individual—and then, dizzied, sat down to write his autobiography. One volume of it was enough for confirmation; he would never write the others. This was the volume in which he wrote about his parents.

Novelty

We have been tested for survival, the biologists say, and not been found wanting. At least we have survived the competition for being born; many others, apparently, would have wished to stand in our place.

A strong argument, this, even with the appeal to vanity that colors a puritan monochrome: we are obliged to prove ourselves before we exist. Life itself is thus a claim of merit, and the evidence for the claim comes from two sides, the first of these with a full hand of examples—opposable thumbs, posture erect, the tongue collaborating with the larynx. Who would have invented these singly, let alone in the conjunction of one body? And there is, in fact, also the evidence from the second side. For although we may at times imagine to ourselves local improvements—a few inches off or on, a sharper, even a third, eye—we do not think here of a different *kind* of body. Even when we wish for wings or claws, the thoughts pass quickly, offspring of circumstance and need. Those changes, we recognize, are borrowed from familiar bodies— birds, tigers—not from figures of our invention.

It seems then that we ought to be content when we cannot imagine an alternative. And in general we do not balk: the body takes up the space of thinking as well as of acting. Thus, it is perversity as much as an impulse of the spirit that leads us all to affect one moment that is in no way bound to survival, that even our genius for procreation has not the slightest chance of transmitting. This invention is sufficiently remote from the probabilities insisted on by life to seem mere chance—were it not for the constancy of its appearances. Admittedly, we should not place much weight on the fact of repetition; it may prove here only how difficult and rare it is to be original even when we aspire to that ideal, even after we acknowledge our special interest in stepping outside the determinations of history and biology.

The only other explanation for death, it seems, is simply curiosity about what stands on the other side. And curiosity, we understand, is still more improbable a quality of nature than originality.

Weather or Not

We do not suppose that people who talk about the weather—
at one time or other, everybody—spend much time thinking
about it. Indeed, the appeal of such talk seems mainly to be
that it does not require thought at all, that it enables the conversation to go on without interruption when our minds are
occupied elsewhere or perhaps when they are just resting. Yet
it is a mistake to conclude from this ready competence that
the talk itself is not serious; we find here rather an easy surface that conceals complex depths, even, at its extreme, a movement of the spirit.

We can hardly avoid encountering this hidden source
once we consider the range of emotions for which the narrow
topic of the weather provides occasion: the span extends from
pleasure to pain, from anger to sorrow, reaching also to ha-
tred and love. This variety, moreover, does not attach itself
with any constancy; defying the law of contradiction, conflicting moods often gather around a single event. If, for example,
rain forestalls a summer outing, this will surely be a subject
for conversation—but if the outing is warmed by clear skies
and a bright sun, or only grudgingly encouraged by clouds
and a too sharp breeze, these too are worth discussing. It is as

if nothing that could happen in the way of weather would diminish our desire to speak of it. Perhaps it is not surprising that we take pleasure in talking about pleasure, but where weather is concerned there seems to be no less pleasure in talking also about pain and disappointment.

If we ask what other topic might be so constant a subject, for better or worse and in good times or bad, the one candidate that comes to mind is money. There, also, we offer tribute to the prices we pay, in their rise and fall or even if they include no change at all. There, too, the range of response is wide, including the feeling of victory that bargains bring, of having for the moment outwitted mortality—and also the sense of loss, of a failing in ourselves, with the discovery of having paid more than we needed to. But in the end money serves conversation less well than weather, since with money we fear the dangers of disclosing how much we have or (almost as bad) of appearing to care for it too much. About the weather, by contrast, we are confident that we speak pertinently, objectively, with full command of the facts and yet also with that rare humility achieved only when a speaker addresses a subject selflessly, disinterestedly. Talking about the weather, moreover, carries an unusual invitation to equality between speaker and listener—the mutual recognition of a competent, even expert, grasp of the subject. In these exchanges, we realize a rare sense of community in a world where separation, partisan division, is a more familiar presence.

Admittedly, it is possible to imagine disruption even in this unusual possibility of fellowship. But the changes required for a breach here are extreme; we can hardly stretch our imaginations to include them. Required would be a person who, facing a bright sky and sun, answers the nominal question, "Nice day, isn't it?" with a frown, adding words of disappointment and then others in favor of fog or rain. It is not only that this person takes the question too literally—it is not really a question, after all—but that his answer moves past the boundaries of a common humanity so that a break is unavoidable, perhaps irreparable. At the very least, that response would be followed by a deep silence — when it is just the threat of such a vacuum that talk about the weather is intended to avert.

The breach threatened here, moreover, extends beyond taste or conventional nicety to the realm of the religious. The sheer *reality* of the weather makes it unique: God himself, it can be argued, hardly affords a presence to equal its inevitability, since even in respect to him there has been questioning and, at an extreme, denial. The skeptics who distance themselves in this way, moveover, have done so at slight cost; some have spoken, with apparent impunity, also about his death. But no such challenges are directed at the weather. We cannot imagine life without it, and people who from the fear of disclosure or confrontation refuse to discuss religion or politics or love speak readily enough about weather, committing themselves openly, without reserve. There is no reason to believe that they are disingenuous or hypocritical in this talk; we should think rather of natural piety, which brings them here not only to believe but to testify.

Together

We have been troubled, even surprised, to learn that institutions often foster the conditions they are meant to overcome. But if we consider the textures of institutions, it becomes obvious that they could hardly avoid this effect. When sick people are brought together under one roof, is it not inevitable—if only from a sense of community—that they will share what they have? And similarly, for criminals in a prison? We should not, then, be surprised to learn that hospitals spread disease, that jails create criminals, that savings banks provoke spending, that schools produce an atmosphere of illiteracy, that restaurants incite hunger, that no infidelity occurs outside marriage. If there is surprise here, it must be in our continuing allegiance to the institutions themselves—the fact that we remain devoted to them when their costs are so great.

The truth is that people can hardly bear to be alone, and so they are willing to pay the price of illness, crime, illiteracy, hunger, bankruptcy, even death—any of these rather than the choice of remaining in solitude. Only an institution that taught people how to live by themselves could counter this failing. As it happens, this is one cure that institutions themselves are unable, certainly unwilling, to provide. And it would hardly be just to fault them in this: how could we require them to be more selfless than people themselves are?

Taking Chances

The theory of probability is a world of intrigue where calculation is its own reward, where the very name betrays a measure of complicity (surely, a fairer, less tendentious title would speak of possibility theory). Those who build castles on its claims for the future openly invite the sands to shift beneath them. I saw this clearly in a friend who, having devoted his life to embellishing the theory, found himself caught between its extremes of actuality and nonexistence—caught, that is, until history made the choice for him.

This friend, who began his career as a political conservative, quickly realized that the theory of probabilities on which he labored conspired with the state to repress the individual. Only if individuals are treated as indistinguishable members of a class, after all, can predictions be made about their common future. But the idea of a class society, my friend claimed (admonishing me, the Marxist), is itself, as idea, an instrument of oppression. If we consider the individual truly as individual, apart from classes, we soon see how unlikely even probability theory itself is. "Is it any more probable that we should be here, talking to each other today, than that I should now fly?" he asked me, beginning his case. "Think of the improbabilities that stand behind us: evolution, the history of language, political institutions, marriage, the unlikelihood of a biological conception, the slight chances of *our* conception. The building we stand in is made of stone from a nameless quarry, accumulated through nameless ages, by nameless and countless agents: the improbability that it should be here is also the improbability that *we* should be here—and even if we give ourselves the benefit of every possible doubt, there is nothing to choose between us. Is history made of parts? Then the parts that are equal as parts are equal to each other in possibility. Do not," he concluded, "take yourself so seriously."

That moral lesson was not lost on me. But despite my efforts, I could hardly have anticipated the use to which my friend turned this now radical plea for individuality, contingency, change. Put it down to pangs of conscience or remorse: there is still no ready way of explaining the contriteness, the penitence, with which he looked back on his own conservative past. "Look," he went on. "Probabilities always remain probabilities, no matter what actually happens; they themselves never become actualities." He noticed my skeptical response with irritation. "Haven't we agreed that before we met here today, the probability that we *would* meet was slight? But there is the same improbability even in our actual meeting. Of course we now look at it as a fact; undoubtedly the other people in the room would do so as well. But if the pieces of the world have probabilities—more precisely, improbabilities—just by being pieces of the world, so then, too, will these facts; they are themselves only possible, not actual. Is there a greater improbability about the unraveling of history—that history will double back on itself, reversing what it had done before—than in its continuing to move in a line? Such a rule would itself be very improbable."

My friend, in the rest of a short and lamented life, celebrated this skepticism, and indeed his commitment to it resulted in large contributions to the theory of culture. Where other, less dedicated thinkers saw only data, numbers, social habits—incest, taboos, language, dress—he saw only permutations of possibility. Conceiving every element of nature as contingent, it was an easy, even a necessary, step for him to view them all as artifacts or forms of language. It was from this basis, for example. that his classic study, "The Genetic Code as Comic Narrative," created the new field of Rhetorical Biology.

His own life, to be sure, suffered predictably from uncertainty and indirection. The severe illness that suddenly came upon him weakened him but even then did not undermine his belief. "The probability that this will finish me—even if it finishes me—is small," he said to me with characteristic assurance during the last visit I had with him. A seizure took him not long after I left, and the gruff doctor who called me on the telephone to tell me the news found no reason to doubt what he had seen.

Doing and Not

There is much interest now in mythological tales of canniness, of how to do things—to fix a car, to smooth a marriage, to find God, to play tennis. We may well understand these as the nostalgia of democratic technology for the traditional and heroic mood of the epic: to every question an answer, for each purpose an instrument, Everyman an Odysseus, adrift in a world of perils where, without notice, anything may stop working. The readers of these instructive tales need not commit themselves to actually *doing* anything; they read the tales as fictions, enlargements of spirit, suspensions of disbelief.

But there is also a different, less subtle side of these careful images of discrimination, since for each set of instructions of what to do, we also hear another, telling us almost in the same voice what to avoid, what *not* to do—and we sense here that technology, far from being a new means, is an old end. Is it not likely that the array of technology, with the meticulous line it draws between what is and what is not to be done, is a reincarnation of the Holy, of that potent line between the Sacred and the Profane? We know that human beings crave difference, contrast—and what readier means is there for satisfying this desire than in the division between what they may and may not do? Difference cannot be more sharply put than by prohibition.

It would hardly be reasonable to blame technology for disguising this spiritual profession as efficiency, for thus concealing its motive. Certainly we have ample warning of this tactic from the history of concealment itself. The mask, after all, the means of reshaping natural appearance, was itself a creation of technology. Indeed, there is some evidence that the mask was its very first achievement, known subsequently, in one of technology's most common forms, as the face. The history of this artifact goes so far back that no one has yet even suggested a date for its invention.

Mirror Images

It takes a lifetime of study to learn the simple lesson that we are responsible for what we do—and to understand this not as an abstract principle or (through pain) as the result of punishment or loss, but in the immediacy of moral conscience. The discovery that motive and act are attached to consequences, that they *cause* them, comes readily enough when we match technology against nature or even when we view the actions of other people; in our own doing or making, however, the awareness comes more slowly. Here, even when we examine conscience closely and painstakingly, press it to the limit in order to see clearly what we do or why—we often find later that also this scrutiny has faltered, since it is the individual who in this labor observes himself, an egocentric reflection that never escapes the temptations and habits of the self, that is, its blindness.

A truer test comes from the view we gain by looking from the outside in—considering not our own consciousness of what we do but the impressions it leaves on the face of the world or, still more expressively, in the faces of those on whom those impressions are made. To be sure, this test, too, may invite distortion: Are not those others also subject to whimsy or habit? And more than this, are they not, also as moral agents, independent of what we could hope to cause in them? Are they not free, in effect, to be arbitrary? But then, we answer, their responses are telling nonetheless: however free they may wish or think themselves, the push that first set them in motion remains inscribed in what they do. Motives, even when strained, count little here: it is the act itself that is displayed, sculpted in the object—much as the artist produces a self-portrait in each painting even when the apparent subject is, more immediately, a Dutch landscape or the Grand Canal of Venice.

Who are these others on whom the marks of our acts are most disinterestedly inscribed? What we look for in answer here is a creation that follows us continuously, that assumes this role without deliberation, without having chosen to involve us—and yet being inextricably linked. It is only so, after all, that what they express would be quite truthful, that what had first set the process in motion would appear as nature itself. There is, I believe, only one of our many achievements or effects in which we are certain of finding this—and that is in our children. In them the mark of family resemblance is unmistakable—often by biology but invariably by moral signature—an effect made the more intense because of the adulthood they soon claim. There, among the many possibilities of growth, a composite appears; like the lines converging from many different impulses and years to make up a single and emphatic face, so *our* actions, constant even when they are hidden, even when we ourselves are unconscious of them, are displayed.

Perhaps you will object that it is not our true or one self that we find outlined in our children, that we are indeed several selves among which the children then choose. Like anyone else who stands in judgment before the court, we too have the right to argue that our children have got it wrong, that the impression they so clearly display of us is not what we are or did, at least not *only* what we are or did. We can say these things and bring evidence; we may attempt to plea-bargain, hoping for a mitigated verdict. But these claims, we will finally have to admit, reflect only possibilities—and the children in whom we face ourselves are actual.

Names

It is the hope of the social sciences to humanize what we would otherwise mistake for nature, thus also to write a social dictionary or lexicon, listing the conventions that shape the boundaries of culture. From one side, names fall readily into line here: French children have French names, Chinese children have Chinese names, and so on. And there are subtler turns as well, starting from the not so obvious premise that since children themselves have nothing to do with what they are named, their names reveal to us their parents—*their* sublimations, hopes: those who think of names as the means of lifting themselves as well as their children from one class to another; who, tethered in a narrow living room, seek exotic and alien lands; who, living in a present without a past, attempt to fill that absence with nostalgia.

But these accounts usually stop short: there cannot be more than this in a name, after all, if language itself is arbitrary, only a set of agreements. Some cultures, however—usually called by us primitive—have thought differently and more deeply about this. These understand that since a name is not only what a person is known by, but also what he knows himself by, the name may also affect what he is or becomes. The one glimpse we allow ourselves of this sophistication is in the deliberate unreality of Hollywood—and there, only in a form that answers to consistency more than to a theory of names: since everything else is appearance, the name must be as well. Novelists, too, occasionally follow this practice in the characters they assign to their fictions; but, again, the method here thrives on consistency, mainly with writers who devote themselves to blatancy, even to caricature. Dickens, for example, with his Murdstones, Pecksniffs, Bounderbys, Scrooges.

We would be better served, I believe, by coming back to life, by taking its alleged artifice as real, its conventions as themselves both affecting and reflecting nature. I confess that this conclusion did not come to me easily, but only under the weight of a group of writers who themselves produced one of the important lexicons for reading human behavior as a text. They thus made it possible to reverse their own means—they, who traced so diligently the artifacts of the mind but who here, against themselves, seemed to find strength in their own names as nature. Should we otherwise think it no more than an accident, mere chance or arbitrariness, that Joy, Young, Rich, Eagle (that is: Freud, Jung, Reich, Adler) converged on a moment?—this gathering of powers that omits nothing that startling accomplishment and heady success might aspire to?

It was soon after recognizing this that I saw what I and others had long been blind to, in a patriarch with even a stronger claim for having disclosed how conventions conceal nature. It is not simply, as we might all agree, that the great critic of capitalist exchange should fittingly have known himself, lifelong, in the form of currency, as Marx: we could hardly even imagine that a new beginning of history would have been summoned in the name of Pfennig. (Nature itself, we learn from these musings, may sometimes be guilty of excess; surely no human writer of fiction would so casually have placed Marx by the side of the Engels.)

Limbs,

Food for Art

🍲

Kafka's tuberculosis undoubtedly would have killed him, but he seems in fact to have died of starvation. The disease had spread to his larynx, and in the last weeks of his life he could hardly swallow; when he died, he weighed about ninety pounds. Also during those last weeks, he corrected the proofs for his story, "The Hunger Artist"; it was published soon after his death. Thus we see in an accidental conjunction the rehearsal of a race that continues to surprise us no matter how many times we see it run, always with the same result: nature, unhurried, seemingly without effort, outstrips the quickened motion of art, the subtleties and turns that the artist strains for in the effort to be original.

We understand, too, that this outcome is not itself an accident. Art, in the end, will always lose to nature, mainly by its dependence on the will, on the choices it constantly requires. To be sure, we defer to art in its heights as the mark of genius: at those moments the artist seems no less free than nature itself. So too, we acknowledge the leap of imagination that brought Kafka to recognize fasting as an art form: the most disembodied of writers concludes that the body itself, so near at hand, so often simply taken for granted, may also be a medium of art.

It might be assumed that this possibility would free the artist, once and for all, for the airy life of the imagination. Yet we know that Kafka, writing his way through lonely midnights, would never stop pondering the weight of his body—in exercise; in the refinements of a diet that took the lemon as a favored delicacy; even in the lightness of sexual intercourse. Kafka would never agree that the imagination sufficed by itself for art, neither his own art nor that of his creations; always there would be the press of conscience—the labor of intending to make something where otherwise would exist only the chance edge of fact. So, too, the hunger-artist, for all the antic genius of his fasting, submitted to constant rehearsal and training; his last and greatest performance—it could only be when he starved himself to death—was carried on selflessly, in the absence of an audience altogether. Nor was the hunger-artist more rigorous or devoted in this commitment than other of Kafka's creations: consider only the patience of Josef K., waiting endlessly for an explanation when the explanation was the waiting itself, or Gregor Samsa, struggling to regain human form when it had been the effort to be human that first turned him into an insect. For them, too, art would begin and end with the will—the imagination only, secondarily, providing a means.

And then, in sharp contrast—nature, disinterested, heedless of other claims to originality, effortlessly but without a hint of the arbitrary, produces a hunger artist in Kafka himself who is more inventive, more fully committed to art than any figure conjured by the human imagination, even when that imagination is Kafka's own. Art conceals art, we often tell ourselves hopefully, but nature, still more the artist, conceals nothing. There was, in the end, nothing other than nature itself to tell; everything that Kafka could be, nature demonstrated that he was.

Here, also, we reach another and more ominous conclusion. For if nature, traversing his life, proved a surer hand at irony than the ironic Kafka, turning him into only another

one of its objects: Can we prevent ourselves from imagining —
what it promises for the rest of us, we who are less honest and
steadfast?

Acrobatics

Like every other fear, the fear of heights has an authentic form that contrasts with many imitations and inauthentic ones. More than other fears, however, the flawed versions of acrophobia rely on conceits and artifice, as though the people who suffer from it must first labor to create it or imagine it themselves. So they require a view from the window of a skyscraper, floors heaped on floors, before anxiety strikes—or they are affected when they find themselves on the edge of a mountain path to which a long journey has led them. So, also, there are those who require the ascent (even by someone else) of a ship's mast, set in the middle of an ocean; or those who wait for the lurch of an airplane before wishing for the comfort of a steady hand to hold the plane tightly in that one place—even, we know, if this means for them that they would not get closer to Chicago for the next day or two.

At these moments, the fear of heights is surely felt as genuine—but it also requires so much in the way of anticipation, such heavy work of contrivance, that it seems less an identity than an expression of vanity: they, small people that they are, have dared to exceed themselves, to challenge space on its own terms. We understand that even success in such an endeavor might well frighten them, take their breath away. But this, for the rest of us, may not be sufficient evidence of authenticity. If those who make the claims really wish to be believed, let them rather find vertigo in the height they reach when they lift their heads from the pillow in the morning. Then even the most skeptical viewers would concede that they were in the presence of despair.

False Immodesty

Why should an elbow show signs of age at all? we might ask captiously, taunted by those symptoms on so many other sides. Elbows hardly suffer from the effects of mental strain, they don't have to worry about finding jobs or paying bills or what their children are doing with their lives. Certainly it is easier, by contrast, to understand the wear and tear on faces: always on display, in motion whenever a conversation is going on, obliged to stay active even when someone else is talking. The heart and the kidneys, too, although hidden, are constantly at work — twenty-four hours a day, seven days a week, an inhuman task really, with no sabbath to look to for relief; it seems forgivable, then, that they should run down or wear out. But elbows have so little *to do*, none of it on their own, almost always subordinate to somebody else, and when they do act on their own, mainly causing blunders or mishaps. Somebody who is all elbows does not advance their cause; "They also serve who only stand and wait" could well have been written about elbows.

Even our usual concerns about appearances, about the impression we make on others, are remote for elbows, since they hardly have to worry about being seen. They are not visible at all from the front—they don't, strictly speaking, *have* a front—so that when they come into view, it is normally from the rear and then at an angle that half conceals them. Yet notwithstanding these advantages, age marks elbows quite deliberately, coarsening their features, inscribing networks of marginal lines and patterns; also their shapes change, much like the body, punctuating bulges and shrinkage where earlier there had been even surface.

With such disclosures, the elbow might seem a symbol of mortality itself: that contract which compels us to recall our status as transients, often at moments when we most wish to stand still, when, like elbows, we might have begun to believe that what we do best is just to stay in one place, without change. Finally, however, such aspirations are illusory, at odds with the character—at best with the truthfulness—of the elbow itself. For although we might at first honor the modesty and self-effacement of elbows, we see in the end that time treats them no less harshly than if they had pushed themselves forward, as though they had chosen to live dangerously, on the edge. And it is difficult, I am afraid, to avoid the suspicion that elbows may themselves be responsible for this inconsistency. Would we not charge hypocrisy to someone who, after leading a placid and subservient, virtually motionless existence, nonetheless pretended to have suffered or endured much?

Admittedly, the accusation of hypocrisy implies that somehow elbows *choose* their appearance, and this may seem a particularly raw example of anthropomorphism. Yet we know also that appearances are never quite accidental, that always behind them, even if at a distance, there is agency and purpose. That we draw this conclusion from experience elsewhere means only that we now find ourselves recognizing a resemblance we had not noticed before—the likeness, I would say, between faces and elbows.

Future Facts

Human eyes are placed in such a way that when the head is in its natural position, they look straight ahead. From this fact, we understand the role that nature has given the neck — perhaps as a concession to the lure of variety, but more probably to allow us an awareness of sides and angles. Even *with* the neck, however, we do not manage to see directly behind ourselves — at least not until the rest of our body also turns (and then, of course, we are not exactly looking behind ourselves). For much of our life, this limitation hardly matters, since we are usually intent on looking forward, not backward. That, after all, is where the future is, with its promise of other beginnings, the occasions of novelty and originality; there, too, is where forgetfulness will occur, or even stronger forms of redemption that undo actions we have been responsible for in the past. All such possibilities stand ahead of us, contrasting sharply with the fixity of the past, its weight of implacability and its indifference to the lure of change. Adventure, after all, is always in the future; it occurs in the past only by revision, often simply by lying.

We understand, then, how serious an alteration it is when people begin in their lives to find themselves looking backwards rather than forwards, when the main possibilities they envisage occur in reflection on the past, in recalling pleasures or pains first learned long before. To be sure, they may enlarge in this way on what might have been, rearranging memory in short sentences of interpretation. But it is the turn itself that is the difference, since the fact is inescapable here that they have changed from looking ahead to looking backwards, focusing—unnecklike—on the landscape behind them.

Changes as large as this occur only as the menace of the future becomes intolerable, when it too begins to take on the features of the past by becoming fixed and implacable. Indeed, in the face of this menace, it is hardly surprising that we might prefer to turn once again to the past; we did, after all, succeed in living through it—something that will not be true of the future. And at some point, no doubt, it requires a quality on the order of heroism to avoid the temptation of this assurance, to continue only to look ahead as the eyes are set. There is the possibility, after all, that by looking backwards we might so increase the flexibility of our necks that we could even, once more, *reach* into the past.

When Freud talked about the patterns of sexual desire, he allowed himself a recognizable wistfulness and nostalgia. But even at their most heated, as they occupied all his thoughts and also, we surmise, his body, he resisted these temptations. There was in him no trace of doubt or illusion about the liabilities of the future, about the cost it would exact: repression, failure, death. And yet it was indeed, always, the future he would face rather than the past. This was, after all, the direction in which nature, his own and nature's nature, was turned. So he would write, in late middle age, confronting the years that pressed on him: "A crust of indifference is slowly creeping up around me, a fact I state without complaining. It is a natural development, a way of beginning to be inorganic." Here there would be no sublimation of the past, no twisting backwards, no regret that the neck could not turn full circle. For the hero, it would be the future, even when it was inanimate, that stirred life in the present.

Marriage and Monotheism

You say that you don't understand why God created Eve, that it would have been in God's own interest to let Adam face the serpent by himself? But surely if there is a question here, it is why God created Adam at all. Once he took *that* step, there had to be Eve in order to make the other half of a couple. This seems to me obvious, and not only on practical grounds — although there, too, we have the part of a reason. The hardest work of creation, we know, goes into the first one of a kind; the second, and the others after it, requires much less effort. It is in fact almost as easy to make two of a kind as to make one, and many artists do just this, often even more than two.

But the issue here is not mainly economics, and we begin to understand this when we recognize that the story of Adam and Eve is not about them at all, but about God; *that*, in fact, is the story. Admittedly this first of all couples catch the reader's eye with their singular creation and then with the way, without actually choosing to remain together, their future is coupled. In all this, God seems hardly active, his presence little more than that of stage director — but this, we find later, is only a stratagem. The director, calling attention to Adam and Eve, still more insistently calls attention to himself and to his own power—first tempting them and then punishing them, first giving them the power of reason and then prohibiting them from using it. And none of this, we learn, is unusual. Whatever happens in the biblical account happens because he wills it; there are no other causes. God himself asserts this repeatedly, and it is not, with him, mere vainglory. He is, in other words, one of a kind, and the *kind*, too—this is the crucial matter—is only one.

It is difficult, in a plural world, with so many like creatures, to imagine what this restriction means. For everything else, in the ordinary way of things, there are always offspring and analogies, often exact replicas—but *here*, in the world on which Adam and Eve imprint themselves and their children, there is to be this one thing that has no likeness, then or ever. (The difficulty of grasping this possibility is best seen in the reluctance of those biblical commentators influenced by Plato, who find themselves moved to the conclusion that a being who is both God and One must then, by that fact, be Two).

Thus, too, we understand more surely why the Bible describes everybody other than God as more than one: such combinations and their collective assembly attest, each time, to God's own difference. Adam and Eve, in fact, are only the first in a long line of couples that demonstrate this. What they assert through drama and the hint of tragedy, for example, Noah's ark proposes more strongly by narration and comedy— for there, too, even with space limited, God would insist that the ark should admit only pairs. The biological explanation offered for this insistence, that the arrangements on the ark answer to requirements of reproduction, is, we recognize, only another example of medical materialism; it begs the question of why God arranged things in *that* way when he could, after all, have appointed three or four sexes, or even only one, rather than two. (The imaginative oyster, we know, took steps on its own in this direction, although with only moderate success; we might wonder in any event whether its androgyny preceded or followed the voyage of the ark).

What is most evident is that the Flood made certain that after it nobody other than God would come in "one's." Thus, Noah's ark, long honored as a symbol of coupling and marriage, serves better, more faithfully, as a testimonial to monotheism in a book that, we conclude, hardly spoke of anything else.

Impotence

Well, Tom, I'm sure that in your reading you come across all kinds of stories. There's probably not much I could tell you that would surprise you, even if I tried to make it up. After all, you're a teacher of literature, and the stories you teach are *all* made up, full of turns and twists that readers would not think of themselves. Anyway, I think of my problem as quite straightforward, not much out of the ordinary, although some people I've spoken to see it as more complicated than that. The fact is—you can recognize how difficult it might be—that I've forgotten how to sleep, quite simply *forgotten* how to do it. Once, of course, I did know how—I did it well; the usual combination of desire and opportunity worked more efficiently for me than it did for most other people. But now all that has gone—except for the memory I have of the pleasure that it gave, the sense of renewal and possibility. I know that I did it, that I had the experience; but no matter how hard I try, I can't seem to remember how to do it.

I recall quite clearly even now the routine I would follow in going to sleep. It would usually be about 11 or 11:30 at night, after a day's work and dinner. I would read for a little while, and then I would go upstairs, use the bathroom, and get undressed. I would lie down on the very comfortable bed I have, piling up several pillows so that my head would be quite high. Then I would turn over on my right side, with my legs bent at the knees, in the same position that I have found comfortable from the time that I was a child. It would usually be a matter of only a few minutes, just of letting my mind wander, and I would be off, sleeping restfully for a full seven or eight hours.

But now something seems always to interfere with that. I go through all the steps I had practiced before—but nothing happens. Everything stays just as it is. My eyes are closed, I'm quite comfortable, nothing has happened to upset me—but still I just lie there, marking time with the hours that go by. Strangely enough, even in the morning afterwards things seem almost normal. I get up as I used to, at about 6:30 or 7 o'clock, shave and get dressed, then I have a bite of breakfast and go on to work. This is all much the same—except that I haven't slept. Usually, I don't even feel too tired, although always I feel regretful, in some way remorseful or guilty, as though I had missed out on something quite important and that this was due to a fault in me.

Friends to whom I've described this pattern tell me that what I have is just another variation of insomnia, but I'm certain that this is not what it is. I once did have insomnia for a couple of months, some years ago, and that was quite different. What would happen then was that I would go to bed upset about an incident at work or after a heavier dinner than I was used to, and I would wake up an hour or two later, unable to continue. Recognizing the cause, however, I would put in a few hours of wakefulness, sometimes reading, sometimes walking around the house a bit; then I would go back to bed as if I were starting over, and soon I would fall asleep again. But that isn't at all the way it is now. This is much more a case, as I've said, of *forgetting*, not of being incapable. Other people are able to do it; I know that at one time I could, too, and I'm certain that I could do it yet if only I had a way to remember.

74

But I can't remember. It's much more like getting on the bicycle I rode every day when I was a teenager and finding that suddenly I no longer knew how to pedal or to keep my balance. I haven't forgotten *those* things, incidentally, and this makes my forgetting how to sleep stranger still. Aside from that one thing, my memory is quite good. Better, in fact, than when I was younger.

Of course, I recognize an irony in what I've been saying: I want to remember how to become unconscious, that is, how not to remember. But as ironies go, this one is mild, something I could live with — although I'm also aware that there is another, easier alternative that I might try. Instead of putting so much effort into remembering what I once knew, I could just try to learn how to sleep all over again — much like what happened, I suppose, the first time round. But you'll have to admit that this would be an unusual project for a middle-aged man, and I don't, in any event, feel up to learning on that scale any more. It would be simpler in every way if I could just remember what I once knew so well. That's why I thought of talking to you, Tom, although I know that the problem of remembering is not usually considered a literary question at all. But it occurred to me that somebody who reads as much as you do might be able to find a story that fits, that you might be able to supply an ending to this one, perhaps only a clue that would jog my memory.

In case you're thinking of suggesting it, I did try once to speak to a psychiatrist about my problem. But that turned out to be an odd experience in itself. Each time I started talking to him about the problem — I went to see him twice a week for a couple of months — I would begin to feel very drowsy, almost falling asleep in his office. Afterwards, at the end of the hour, I would be wide awake again. The fact that I had relaxed a bit in his office didn't make any difference, either, when I tried to go to sleep that night; evidently I had not learned anything that I could use on my own. And the truth is that I don't believe that what's bothering me is a psychological problem at all; I really *do* want to fall asleep—it's an object of great desire for me, not of fear or anxiety.

The psychiatrist once suggested that sleep might have certain symbolic associations for me, but neither he nor I could figure out what they were. Sleep doesn't have much shape to it, after all, and I'm past the point in life where I deny myself things just because I want them. The psychiatrist himself said, when I was leaving for the last time, that on balance I seemed pretty well adjusted; we parted more as friends, in fact, than as doctor and patient. He did mention that we could continue talking, that we might discuss other things—but he wasn't at all confident that we would be able to recall the past clearly enough for me to remember how to sleep. And since it was this that was bothering me, I thought I should concentrate on it; so we shook hands, and he wished me good luck. It was after this that it occurred to me that perhaps I had been looking in the wrong place, that you might recall something writers had imagined that could bring my past into the present. Isn't there a book I could find myself in? Because then I might be able to read myself to sleep . . .

Nature's Nature

When someone walks for the sake of walking and not merely to get someplace, there is a point at which the walker "hits his stride," discovering the natural pace that apparently holds itself in waiting inside every pair of legs. (This applies not only to humans, although it is less surprising to find it in animals or insects. Try to imagine, for example, a centipede that had *not* hit its stride . . .) I have at times speculated about what this impulse does with itself when it is not let loose: is it impatient, fidgeting to get out? Does its frustration turn in other directions — for example, putting ideas of sexual adventure in the nonwalker's mind, or dreams of motion in his sleep? Does it find outlets of sublimation — perhaps an ideology that justifies motionlessness? The pressures hardly disappear even if a person does start walking, but not in his stride. "So near and yet so far," we can hear the pace within the walker complaining; "Why won't he just give in?"

Walking may not seem important enough to warrant a campaign on nature's behalf — but that same stride, the rhythmic pace that nature has settled on, seems in fact to extend farther than only to the legs. Is it so implausible to guess that for every person there is a structure that marks the convergence of all his impulses, providing a single measure of what resides there, in the person, waiting to be let out? We do not usually think of ourselves in this way because we tend to believe that we choose to do what we do, or (as a last resort) that we are compelled to it by some external force—never because nature's nature is only expressing itself. Living constantly by technology, we subtract from nature the power we ascribe to man. To change this, we would have to see artifice and training as expressive or natural, and this would be a difficult change to make, especially as it applies to ourselves. But the evidence, it seems to me, is undeniable.

Consider this. I have a friend who spends his working days teaching and writing as a professor of English history. In that work he is highly competent, respected by his colleagues and admired by his students; his books have given him a reputation among many readers who do not know him personally. Fair in his use of evidence, resourceful in his imagination, it is his profession that occupies him, not the other way round. Yet I who know him well also know that it is when he is driving his car—for that matter, any car: it is the driving that counts—that his self is most at home in its center, that his dispositions fit most harmoniously together. He feels the need for continuous activity—and driving, of course, provides that. But he needs to be able to rise above or even to leave whatever activity engages him, at the same time to do it and to recognize a world beyond it—and driving is close enough to a routine to be done with only half a mind, leaving the other half free to wander someplace else. He enjoys anticipating contingencies, predicting them, or averting them—and the landscape of driving offers opportunities for all of these. He longs for but rarely gets quick responses to his requests—and cars offer that; he enjoys following well-laid-out paths rather than breaking trail—and again, driving provides a sanction for this; he craves the power, at each moment, to compel someone else to do exactly what he wishes, and cars provide just that measure of sovereignty. You can understand from these requirements why teaching or writing history would be a less genial source for my friend than driving; it offers some of these possibilities, but always with qualifications or conditions.

I'm certain, by the way, that my friend is not aware of this discrepancy. He undoubtedly thinks of his pleasure in driving as trivial—irrelevant to matters of importance and not even central to his pleasures. If I were to tell him what I've just told you, he would think it was a bad joke, something I had cooked up, perhaps from envy at the success of his career; in any event, he wouldn't believe it, and he certainly would not thank me. So nature always makes its presence known— but not necessarily to him whose nature it is.

The Art of Cruelty
❦

The differences between brutality and cruelty hardly matter to their victims: pain, suffering, death come from either. But for the agents who cause them or for anyone who observes them, the differences are unmistakable: cruelty with its impress of imagination, refining the extent of pain's possibilities—contrasted with brutality, which reflects only the will to act, or more simply, to have one's way. This difference entails the awkward consequence that cruelty is more distinctively human than brutality, requiring a certain expansiveness of spirit. Even then, to be sure, the distribution is uneven: some people are better able than others to see around the present into the future. With that ability, they subordinate memory to desire, refusing to settle for the brute facts that would otherwise govern them as well as others.

And certainly, through the long history of cruelty—predictably in the fine discriminations of torture, but also in the varieties of civil punishment and the duress of international war; more generally, in man's *progress* at devising new instruments of suffering—there is no doubt that this history, like the milder histories of painting or poetry, is infused with imagination, an impulse for originality stirred by the prospect of undiscovered openings to the future.

80

We find here, in fact, the familiar lure of art—a desire for beauty's passionate symmetry. In cruelty, this desire discloses itself in the effort to match the instruments that cause suffering and the parts of persons on which they act: the ideal is of a perfect fit, to make the two sides seem (as they would then be) "made" for each other. Admittedly, this goal is an inversion: so to controvert the parts that make up a person (limbs, nerve endings, emotions, thoughts) that the pain caused by the touch of their precise opposites has the clear intensity of spirit. And this reasoned quality of cruelty is not only possible but necessary, since the pain would indeed have first been conceived in the agent's mind and only then asserted in the victim.

Because of this genealogy, it is almost impossible that cruelty should ever even appear accidental. And indeed, to experience or observe it is to be driven by an argument from design to the existence of a source that first deliberated on the possibility of an act and then chose to do it. Thus cruelty is a function of mind, not of body; and the implication would follow that although nature is openly brutal in many of its arrangements—the wolf tearing the throat out of the deer, the eagle snatching the lamb into a depthless sky—to describe such rudimentary events as acts of cruelty would be a serious error of judgment. The deer and the sheep have had their food; so too (it is almost a matter of justice) the eagle and the wolf shall have theirs. And although the loser in these encounters must have been hardly less canny or industrious than the winner in order to have survived that long (is it only the ability to put their heads down and find food that makes sheep sheepish— or because they are sheepish that nourishment comes so easily?), the calculations made by the predators who win out are obviously not *meant* to produce suffering. We find here only a clash of desires: brute force brutally engaged and then brutally concluded.

Thus nature *seems* innocent of the charge of cruelty, its apparent calculation of utility not an act of imagination at all—

rather a gesture of will and prudence, with its practical motives fixed and discernible. Yet as we examine nature less superficially, less dramatically, certain evidence of cruelty also appears there that in fact outstrips not only what chance might accomplish but anything the human imagination could contrive; the source must, it seems, be both deliberate and larger than life. There, in any event, *brute* nature affords no explanation; we might better ask — as if standing in the eye of a hurricane or resting between tremors of an earthquake — what the dimensions of the human imagination would be when joined to the power of nature.

In these cases, nature acts as human inventiveness could not (*would* not, giving human nature the benefit of the doubt) — and yet in ways that are unmistakably the result of design, impossible to comprehend as chance or the result of mere instinct. Few people who have met life close-up, in the flesh, will be unfamiliar with this argument from design, whether through harsh lessons they have themselves learned or by accounts that they have heard. If even one of every ten such stories were collected in an anthology of cruelty, that book would stretch its readers' endurance to the limits; certainly, the volume itself could never be read cover to cover.

I recently heard an account that I quickly (too quickly, as I found) settled on as my own contribution to this anthology, harsh and sharp-edged as I thought any entry to be found there might be. A woman in her mid-forties — in the midst also of family, career, promise — suddenly found herself to be dying of ovarian cancer. It only happened (so the more usual retelling would have it) that at the same time, with the two diagnoses and prognoses — the two bodies — closely coordinated, the mother of this woman was also dying, also in full and painful consciousness, of the same (or, at least, the common) disease. Mother and daughter, daughter and mother: each knew of her own and the other's condition.

In hearing this, it seemed evident to me that however one allowed for brutishness in nature, such expert symmetry could hardly be the effect of a spontaneous or mindless impulse. Would not an intelligence or, more to the point, an imagination be required for such harmonious attunement? Think only of the conjunction of likeness and difference: the shared site of illness having served for birth and individuation—the two generations then converging on a single end, joining mother and daughter in common pain and then a new but still common history. Is there a reasonable alternative here to the supposition of design?

I knew that in urging this conclusion, I risked anthropomorphism, perhaps falling victim myself to the pathetic fallacy that ascribes consciousness to inanimate objects. I knew, too, that the improbabilities in the story might seem sharper than they actually were, because they had been condensed in the telling; the fuller history could well disclose more diffuse, even incidental, possibilities. In the face of such criticism I might have faltered, perhaps even given up the claim for a designing intelligence—if not for a second account that I heard soon after the first and that seems to me still to preclude even the most delicately nuanced doubt about an intentional source for nature's cruelty.

Here also appears a threat to the common assumption that limits themselves have a limit, a warning that just when we feel certain that we have reached the bounds of the imagination, the imagination itself may prove us wrong. Consider now this: A woman in her late thirties, long desirous of home and children, had married and found soon afterward that she was pregnant. After several months, she experienced an unusual abdominal pain. Her doctor's first nonchalance gave way to tests, then to hypotheses, and then to a conclusion. The woman was still pregnant (now, after all the examinations, in her seventh month). But she also bore a virulent cancer that the pregnancy had concealed and that, the medical staff judged, allowed her (then) between one and two months of life. Her new physical pain could be moderated only by drugs that would harm the baby; the woman ruled these out. The effects

83

of the earlier exploratory operations, it was decided, made a Caesarean section necessary for the baby's delivery. In order to allow the baby to come to full term, the delivery would also come close to the time anticipated for the mother's death. And then this last condition was itself intensified: it was virtually certain that the procedure of the Caesarean section, necessary to deliver the baby alive, would kill the mother.

The last of these stipulations appeared not as an option but a prediction. And here, I believe, there can be no question of spontaneous irony or chance occurrence, certainly not of a role for an unknowing or heedless nature. The connections affecting the path of causality are too intricately woven, too minutely asserted, for an unthinking source to have been responsible. Perhaps nature's sometime randomness cannot be ruled out as logical possibility; but as explanation, this recourse seems foolish, a grasping at scientific straws—in comparison to the alternative of an imaginative act that first artfully conceived the possibilities of inversion and then chose among them. The most hardened skeptic will, I believe, find it difficult not to soften here; the causal network in the story is so dense, so much sturdier than the usual evidence cited for the existence of a cosmic machinist or clock-winder: to refuse to admit a being responsible for its art seems itself unbelievable. The one assumption required here—one we otherwise make on much weaker evidence for the sake of either science or religion—is for the existence of a larger-than-human imagination.

Admittedly, in considering this version of nature's cruelty, we would still not understand why any such larger-than-life imagination would have willed into existence what it first only conceived as possible. But our inability to answer this question should not turn the occasion of the question into bliss or suggest to us that the cruelty we recognize is only apparent. We can, in fact, hardly avoid imagining the imagination of evil at work here: finely tuned, deliberate, with a sure eye for balance and fit—and then, too, with the will to see the imagined possibility of cruelty through to its end.

Anyone who requires more evidence for this verdict than a rehearsal of the events themselves has only to turn to Voltaire's deliberately crude appraisal. One can, he concedes, think of objections to a claim for the existence of a being responsible for nature's acts. But the only alternative to that claim is in a brute and unknowing nature, one that moves by chance. And the burden of accepting this alternative is more than difficult (he spoke here without thinking of cruelty at all), it is absurd.

So nature's artifice—or is it God's?—once again overtakes human ambition.

A Bildungsroman

The young boy had obligations pushed on him early—to his widowed and solitary mother, to his studies, to the demands of religious practice. So he learned early to think first of what he ought to do and only then to consider what he wanted to do. This pattern continued through much of his life, and it was at the brink of desperation, looking out at failure in work and friends, brought on by his constant efforts to do what he ought and the realization of never quite fulfilling it, that he one day, without warning, recognized that it might be possible to think first about what he wanted and only then of what he ought to do (that is, what others thought he ought to do). But handicapped by his past, he quickly discovered that he had to *learn* to think about what he wanted to do, giving to the process a concentrated act of the imagination. He took on the task conscientiously, however, and he had just begun to reach certain conclusions about what he did want when he discovered that time was up. He had finally managed the thinking; the doing would now have to wait for someone else.

The Fail-Safe Principle

There was once a man who observed the fail-safe principle in marriage. Although his wife was devoted to him and his children were relatively trouble-free, he also saw in them reason to fear that if a time came when he could not serve them as they were used to, he might find himself left alone, with no one to rely on. So, in the interests of prudence and also to compensate himself for having *to be* prudent—for these reasons, and still more because he found in her an unusual passion, he became involved in a secret but constant relationship with another woman who saw the world so clearly, with him in its foreground, that he knew he could count on her for help and truths that he might not yet even imagine. If, the man said to himself, I need her more than I do now, she'll be there; if I need her only as much as I do now, she is there. And so it was—she was there. The one thing that the fail-safe principle could not provide, he also knew, was a true marriage; contingency, after all, is not actuality.

(He might also have been mistaken about the fail-safe principle: perhaps he could rely on the second woman for support only as long as he did not have to apply to her. Could this even be the reason she was attracted to him? The answers to

87

these questions, of course, he would never know beforehand. He recognized, however—with a sense of both relief and discomfort—that a second fail-safe measure, intended to shore up the first, would provide no greater assurance.)

Redress

SHE: Would you *please* stop staring at everyone's breasts?

HE: It's not everyone—it's just the women.

SHE: That's what I mean. The whole thing is very embarrassing—it embarrasses them, and it embarrasses me.

HE: They don't seem to mind it, as far as I can tell. All that I do, really, is look at their faces, only lower down. As if I had a problem with my eyes and had to look at an angle about 10° below whatever it was that I wanted to see.

SHE: But why would those women think you had a problem with your eyes? They'd be more likely to think that you were just staring at their breasts.

HE: Well, what if they do? The breasts are there, after all, and you only have to try looking at a woman without seeing them to find out how far you can get. Furthermore, they're interesting: so many shapes and sizes, and with such different ways of presenting themselves—some attempting concealment, some clearly on display, some quite artless—and each of these in an effort to be seen without seeming to be seen. I can almost always tell what the woman is from the breast, even when it's inside a dress or sweater, even a coat. That would be reason enough to be interested, even if it weren't also erotic. Why *shouldn't* I stare?

SHE: You make it sound like science when it's not knowledge you're after at all. You look at breasts because you want to touch them and you can't; and *that* shows in your look. That's what makes the staring embarrassing.

HE: Well, it's not as if breasts don't like to be touched, is it? Or more exactly, that they don't like to be almost touched, or even more precisely, touched without being touched. That's what looking is, after all: touching without touching. What you think of as embarrassment or self-consciousness is only anticipation, a suspicion of pleasure. In all the years I've been staring, no one has ever protested. Doesn't that mean something?

SHE: It means only that you're never quite open about it. You move your eyes around a bit, back and forth or up and down—just enough so that if some woman was braver than usual and challenged you, you could pretend not to know what she was talking about. You'd probably act indignant, as though *she* had insulted *you*.

HE: Yes, but you see, I go through all that as much for them as for me. If I stared without covering it up at all, they'd feel they *had* to say something about it. This way we both have the pleasure: me of almost touching, them of almost being touched—and neither of us has to worry about being caught.

SHE: That's another thing—*what* pleasure? You talk of touching without touching. Suppose you could *actually* touch instead of staring. You look all the time—when you cross the street, when you're waiting at the counter in a store, when you're sitting on the bus. Any pair of breasts will do, the more the better. It's not only that you don't make any distinctions; I'm talking about capacity. What pleasure can there be in touching constantly, almost without interruption? After a while, it wouldn't make any impression at all.

HE: But that's just the difference between seeing and touching: with seeing, the impressions and pleasure never stop. Unlike other parts of the body—even, Flaubert said, his heart—the eye doesn't know what impotence is. And anyway, sexual pleasure is not the only reason for staring: you're the one who fixed on that. You remember Hillary's answer when they asked him why he'd climbed Everest? "Because it was there!" he said. Well, there are mountains and then there are mountains . . .

SHE: That all sounds very high-minded, but it doesn't fool me for a minute. *I* remember Willie Sutton's answer when the police asked him why he kept on robbing banks after he'd been put in jail a few times. "That's where the money is," he said—and if you were telling the truth, *you'd* say something like that about breasts. I'd almost rather see you interested in money. Anyway, how do you think it makes me feel when we're walking together and I know that you're doing this to every woman we pass. It's not a question of fidelity—although I wouldn't be surprised if deceit begins first in the eyes. It's more a matter of your not being present when you're pretending to be. At the same time we're talking, your mind is running back and forth, checking out these or those, figuring out how much more you might see from what angle, taking time off from listening to imagine the invisible, measuring shape and size, comparing and contrasting—all while you're keeping up your side of conversation about Iraq or the economy.

HE: Well, well, I admit that. But most other people do more than one thing at a time, and at least these two are very different kinds of things—looking and talking. It's not as if I'm *thinking* of anything else when I'm talking to you. Anyway, you've often said that you like me best when I'm giving you my divided attention; why the rush of jealousy about this?

SHE: I meant your sense of irony—but there's nothing ironic in the difference between your talking and your staring. It's much closer to hypocrisy, the words coming as a smoke screen to cover something else.

HE: Well, if it's honesty you want, I'll be glad to try it— although I'm not sure, in looking at breasts, exactly how to go about it. What should I do? Look but not think? Not look but think? Not think and not look? It might turn out, you know, that my eyes have a mind of their own . . .

Eros Unbound

The audience had not yet settled down. Chairs were still scraping and papers were still rustling. The speaker's first sentences were weak, barely audible; only the words that he spoke with special emphasis — brief in themselves — reached the audience: "Love," the speaker said, and the rest of the sentence seemed a single, long and garbled syllable. Gradually the large hall became still, and the muted, high-pitched voice that before had been diffident gained energy from the silence. "Love," the speaker said, evidently for the second time, and now the words following it could be heard clearly, "is not a practical need of man, but the result of a decision and an act of the imagination. I have claimed in the past, on evidence that I believe still to be valid, that this strongest of ties among human beings is not due to the incentive of practical necessity, nor even, more simply, to the desire for pleasure. These are relevant, no doubt, but they do not explain the commitments that often link people to each other and on which they constantly act, to the extent — more often than they may themselves realize — of causing them to sacrifice their lives. For such decisions, there is no practical need and certainly no desire; indeed there could hardly be awareness of the possibility before the fact itself. Furthermore, even for love that does begin with practical need—in the physical dependence of a child on a parent, for example—we know that something that starts in this way often reaches beyond the need itself, inventing as it goes, contriving a quite different result.

"All this, I realize, is known to you. But now, with certain regrets, yet without doubting that it must be said, I have something to add to the line of argument established in this fashion. For if, at a first stage, we recall the contention that love is a fulfillment of egoistic needs—two separate selves seeking each other out; and if, in the second stage, we recognize that an additional sense of sympathy or altruism is required to explain the selflessness and sense of commitment that love sometimes achieves, I have now concluded that we must also face the test of a third stage that goes beyond these.

"Think, my friends, of this possibility. Imagine that the pleasures associated with love—and no one, from Plato to Spinoza to Marx, has doubted that pleasure is a feature of love, whether in sexual love, the moral love of pure friendship, or the intellectual love of God—imagine what would happen to these valued relations if the pleasure associated with them were suddenly replaced by pain. Which of these relations, how much of any of them, would survive this change? Would generosity, the altruism of one member of a group to others, outlast a special and constant injection of pain? Even the relationship between the best and closest of friends would be tested by this. And think further, also, of the existence of our dear children: suppose now that pain was now to be a feature not only of their birth, but that they were also, before that, *begotten* in pain, pain that unlike the curse first set against Eve, made itself felt in the climax of intercourse. Which of the ideals of community and fellowship, the love of continuity, of culture, the commitment to a collective identity—those ideals of which children and the family are the very basis—which of these would withstand such an alteration?"

There was, following this question, a sharp silence, as

though an answer to it were imminent. But instead, the speaker started up again. "It is obvious, moreover, that only if we risk this third step can we discover what we have set ourselves to learn about the nature of love. Without such knowledge, anything we say now provides a description of love only as we happen to find it—not an explanation at all. Only by considering this new possibility can we determine whether love is a good at all, chosen for itself and not instrumentally, for other and selfish reasons.

"I myself believe that this third step, too, may yet establish love as an ideal—that the question we now pose for it does not, as enemies of our science have long maintained, drive us back to the egoistic theories according to which pleasure and pain determine our actions in all that we do. But I am obliged also to confess that, as yet, the experiments I have developed for testing this third step are rudimentary. I have yet to find a way of distinguishing people who enjoy pain and who might then value love *because* of the pain it causes—from those who would continue to value love *despite* the pain that this new arrangement leaves room for. For the people of the latter sort, it would be evident that also pleasure—in its earlier time—had not been their motive, or at least not all of it. In finding a basis for this distinction, my friends, lies the hope not only of a theory of culture but probably of the existence of culture itself. And I ask you now—I do not myself have much more time to give to it—to join me in attempting to discover the means for such a proof. I need not tell you, beyond what I have already said, what importance the answer would have for our common work."

The lecturer, who had spoken without notes and so had no gesture of conclusion to make at the end of this last sentence, began to walk slowly toward the side of the stage. He had almost reached it before the audience realized that the lecture was over. A sudden murmur arose then, but the speaker moved steadily off the stage without looking backward and with no indication that he heard.

Spectator Sex

When we hear that beauty is in the eye of the beholder, we understand this to mean not that the eye is beautiful, but that the eye sees other objects as beautiful; without its contribution, the objects would not *be* beautiful, although in contrast they would still, unseen or seen, continue in themselves to be round or square, have a certain weight. The hackneyed phrase asserts, then, that where beauty is concerned, the eye is bound by no constraints or rules; it is itself the court of last appeal, able — obliged — to indulge every impulse, writing off the most extreme disagreements as matters only of inclination or taste.

This description of the eye seems to me false; indeed, it verges on libel, although I also understand the reluctance of the eye to defend itself. The principal testimony available on its behalf joins two subjects that, although freely spoken about separately, evoke a certain hesitation when joined. Sex and age, the two are — and the evidence they provide goes like this: In the usual run of things, the eye calls the attention of the sexual organs — that is, invites desire — to other people of approximately a like age, expanding its own sense of possibility as the years themselves progress. The eye, in other words, at once measures and incorporates the passage of time. Could any boy of fourteen or fifteen, for example, ardent in his first love, even imagine that thirty years later he would have as strong a desire for a woman the age of his girlfriend's mother? Yet the fact remains—and although it is not only the eye that alters in thirty years, the other changes would not matter, would not seek an outlet, unless the eye, that pathfinder, were engaged in the conspiracy. Beauty, in other words, has two centers, one in the object, including there its mark of age, the other in the eye of the beholder—literally *in* the eye—as desire stirs. What beauty is *not*, at any rate, is the expression of whimsy or impulse. Time, and then also its adherent, beauty, are no less matters of fact than other historical occurrences.

I am aware, to be sure, of evidence that might be summoned against this theory: the sometime passion of age for youth, or conversely (a more serious objection), the attraction that youth occasionally finds in age. But I do not mean to deny the possibilities of inspiration or inventiveness: they do not, in any event, affect the general rule. For there the lesson is plain: we desire not what we choose to but what we are able to, in a strict sense what we have to—the eye (our eye) discovering the object to us. Even then, of course, desire cannot always be turned into act, but this is not because the eye is impotent. It will have done everything that an eye could be expected to; other organs of the body must be responsible for themselves.

The explanation has sometimes been given that this expanding horizon that adds new beauty to old with the passage of time testifies to the growing tolerance of age: that age thus leaves behind the prejudices and sharp exclusions of youth. But the evidence seems to me weighted heavily on the other side, calling attention to what we recognize, by contrast, as the impatience of age: when the range of sexual attraction expands, tolerance in general decreases. This too, it will be noted, is proof that beauty ascribed to the eye of the beholder is literally—physically—*in* the eye: as it increases, there is less and less room left for anything else.

Sins,

Choosing

Ask any ten people what fruit brought their downfall to Adam and Eve in the Garden of Eden, and you will hear ten stories, perhaps different in other ways, but each about an apple. Yet there was no apple, or at least we have no reason to believe that there was; the Book of Genesis, the chronicle of the history, speaks only of "fruit." And thus, a question that asks more about human imagination than about history: Why should we, readers, editors, and redactors, have invented the story of an apple? Certainly, as we put ourselves in the way of this doubt, we can readily imagine the same temptation, but with other possibilities: the golden orange, challenging, in Eve's eye, the sun; the ripe dark fig, bursting with seed; the oval, thus directional, pear; the banana, hiding under the lure of skin; the more than bite-sized pineapple, the plum, the date. Which of them could not have served the purpose of the serpent? We know enough of Eden to know that they all would have been present.

The apple, in other words, has been our choice—not, as far as we know, the serpent's, or Adam's, or Eve's. And here, no doubt, we carry on the work of a quite different account in the Bible of sin and guilt. In it there is a measure of bitterness and deviousness beside which the first disobedience and lies of Eden seem naïve, almost innocent.

How else should we describe this, when our choice of the apple turns out to be another episode in the lengthy, still imminent history of the scapegoat?

A Fit Crime

And what if the idea of punishment preceded, not followed wrongdoing? See how we accept one piece of the temporal order as the whole: first, crime — then, punishment. But for the species, at its beginning, this history is reversed: first, the prohibition, the legislation of punishment — and then the crime.

Looking backwards, one can easily understand this relation of cause and effect: prohibitions breed temptation even when their objects would not. (There could have been nothing special, after all, about one piece of fruit in the midst of a large and ripe garden.) Temptation, desire, starts from the sense of mingling: the look here and now at something itself alien, distanced. Desire becomes stronger, more urgent, as not the one, but the two sides of the prospect are real. Punishment, then, has at least the attraction of reality, and not only for the masochist: few moments in the net of experience are more decisive than pain. Even mere names draw on this power of ratification. Call someone a criminal — and it requires in that person rare asceticism not to give a part of himself to the name. Those who believe that titles or names are tokens of a world already fixed invoke the myth of a linguistic paradise. When the criminologist tells us, then, that a thief who is caught is more likely to repeat his crime than one who is not caught, we may object that he could know this only by magical vision—yet we believe him anyway. Why should thieves—*anyone*—not live out the role that society, with its machines and weights, gives them?

One important question, however, is left by this understanding. For if, historically—anthropologically, psychologically—prohibition and punishment precede crime, we can no longer claim that they have been designed to deter crime, not even, more simply, that they are meant to right the balance of injustice. What remains of their origin, in fact, is precisely the lack of a cause—testimony to the lure of absence, and then to the difference between man and nature. Thus we understand that in a world where everything is permitted, where everything is given, something would yet be missing: the lure of prohibition.

We see how powerful this attraction can be when we realize that God himself has not been exempt. Certainly he gave no reason for bringing prohibitions into the world; the first one, placed in Eden together with its limitless nature, is not even named among his creations. It is reasonable to suppose that he did not want to be questioned about this, that God himself also desired desire.

The Marriage Paradox

Paradoxes in logic often only tease the mind; it is when they affect the body that we recognize the impossibility of being in two places at the same time and in the same respect. I can imagine a marriage that stays together only because one or both of its partners fear the violence of divorce—the thrusts, the shouting, the recriminations, insults, threats—mainly because those wounds are already familiar. For the same reasons, in other words, that divorce is desired in the first place. And where any two prospects of pain are equal, it is the one already actual that wins. Thus we see here a practical paradox, followed quickly by a moral one. The practical paradox is that the same causes that make a person's married life painful make the prospect of ending it impossible. The moral paradox is subtler but deeper: a husband or wife, afraid of proposing divorce, intimidated by the likely effects of insisting on his or her suffering, chooses to live with that pain rather than face the attempt to be free of it—at the same time willing, as the one possible means of escape, the death of the other.

"Have you ever thought of divorce?" a pastor, listening once again to a narrative of marital pain, thinks to advise the parishioner who has come to him. "Divorce, no—murder, yes," the innocent answer comes. And the pastor then recognizes both the limits of courage and the boundlessness of advice.

The Genius of the Lie

At one time in my life, I knew two men, quite different in appearance (the one tall, thin; the other short, bulky, meso-morphic), but both adept at the art of deception; together they marked out, once and for all, the limits of that art. I myself undertook to demonstrate their genius to the world through a subtle and exhaustive test. For a month, waking and sleeping, dreaming or conscious, speaking and silent, they were moni-tored by detectors that, by a network of physiological sensors, measured every statement they made as truth or falsehood. As a result of those tests, both men became public figures; also, when the results of the tests became known, their private lives suffered and required rearrangement.

The first of the men made statements that were the most patent, self-contradictory lies — he was given, for one thing, to proclamations about his sexual prowess (often with women he had never met) and about the number of women (some of them the same ones) who, he claimed, had loved him not sexu-ally but spiritually. These assertions nonetheless registered on the lie detectors always as true: he had, evidently, fully con-vinced himself and made his flesh conform to his will.

The statements of the second man, who was more open

and less refined in his genius, were in certain respects still more intriguing; they registered always as false. In this they could not have represented anything less than an unusual moral commitment, an enormous humility. For the characteristic of lying showed up not only in statements he made in the course of his work as a mathematician (he had himself been responsible for a number of original proofs); even on much simpler matters—when he gave his name and address to the clerk at the post office—the detector found that his statements registered always as deceptions.

Someone, doubting the latter finding, requested that the testing apparatus itself be reexamined. This was done, but most of us knew, even before the results of the examination came out, that the machine was not culpable. It had been the premise of our investigation, after all, that lying was human, that machines were not that far advanced.

Losing Paradise

The impulse to seek pleasure probably does not explain all human conduct (love, for example, seems often to welcome pain, to thwart pleasure). But if we ask about the attraction of lying, we do well to start with pleasures promised: the debt skirted for the sake of profit; the boastful lie in the desire for status; the small denial to avoid recrimination. And with this we may guess that only greater pleasure as an alternative, or pain as a consequence, would lead to avoiding the lie itself. I do not know much about these alternate pleasures (they might be only other, even larger, lies) — but I can easily imagine a greater although perhaps unfelt pain.

Think first of the conditions that accompany lying — one, in particular, that the liar would hardly be able to do without: the ability to remember the lie he tells. For without this memory, much of the pleasure would be gone. The lie to the tax collector? — how would the liar gain from it if he could not remember his profit? The denial of an action? — but the pleasure is more than doubled, we suppose, when the liar preserves for himself both the knowledge of guilt and the appearance of innocence. And then: one has to remember the truth as well as the lie in order to bring consistency to a recriminatory future.

Few actions are without consequence; where lies can be so many things other than the truth, their tracks must first be clear in order to be covered later. Even confession or atonement, after all, require memory of what the lie was: to confess to the sin of lying without naming it only reserves the lie itself for later repetition.

And here, through all this, immediate or prospective, the liar himself lives by a mistake, an intentional mistake — in other words, a lie. He believes always that he preserves himself, that at least his memory of his actions is clear. Truth to one side, unpleasant, abrasive; falsehood, to the other side, easy, submissive. It is a myth of distance that the liar employs here, the image of a false but honest consciousness contrasted with a true but dishonest will. But this cannot be. For we know or at least guess that memory is not detached from desire, that memory, too, is constructed, piece by piece, item by item. And then we also recognize that the memory on which the liar is so fully dependent, what he remembers *with*, has itself been built of the stories he tells.

There may indeed be liars who even if they knew that these were the stakes would be willing to sacrifice themselves, willing to barter the past, perhaps to deny it; we ought, no doubt, to respect such single-mindedness and dedication. But it is not easy to know how to declare our respect or where to present it, because the liar rarely sits still. Indeed, the one and only fact we know about the liar is that he tells his first lie to himself — when he tells himself he will remember the difference between the truth and the lie he is going to tell.

Children and Adults

Vice and virtue are usually opposed to each other as if each were only one thing. But although there may be one way to be good or to do right, there are many ways to do wrong; this, rather than ignorance or the will to cause harm seems, in fact, to be the attraction of evil.

And so, also, not least, with adultery, as it is counted among the large and destructive vices. Adult adultery and child adultery, I call two of these varieties. In the first adultery, of children: the act is committed for another end, to rectify the past, if only in pleasure, and thus to address others as well as oneself. The principal future for such adultery, of course, is disclosure: the original privacy of the act is later consummated openly, as others come to know of it, sometimes are *made* to know. This is a way, after all, to public status, to pain, and to the dissolution of marriage (not any one marriage, but all marriage) — ends foreseen and to that extent willed by most human beings.

And then there is adult adultery, which comes close, by the inversion of history that we preserve as irony, to the traditional ideal of marriage: two become one, not by man to be put asunder. A commitment so hedged by circumstance that the adulterers are aware (even those who do not spontaneously think of death) that the relation, the act, will die with them, known only to them, valued by the two of them alone. No progeny, no witnesses. The passion they have for each other can never be fed by looks from outside that spur on most human efforts—not approval, not disapproval, not even mere curiosity. The history of the relation is entirely internal: no letters, no traces (for historians, it would not be history at all). Seclusion is a condition for openness between the pair; disclosure would make the passion impossible. So this adultery is held aside, in a space and time severed from the world; the cuts remain always open, the bruising of touch is their one but constant reminder of the world's body. The one possible breach in this relation is that the two people may come to think of it as a dream. Then, too, of course, they would not be separated, and some couples have even preferred to think of themselves in this way.

(I do not deny a third possibility, the adultery of piety —where one person gives himself to another with no hope or expectation of return. It is an adultery of humility, this; there is nothing to be known or disclosed, for there is no act of joining—only the opening of a self; there is no assurance even of the impression it leaves. Few people are capable of such giving; few are able to be recipients, moving neither to invite nor to direct, still less to take. There is a reasonable question whether these figures should be called adulterers at all: the one obviously has no commitment to violate, the other deprives marriage of no bond.)

Partial Recall

John said to Jane, "Let's forgive and forget. I explained to you what I did and you told me why you did what you did. I think that you were wrong, and you probably still think that I was wrong. Let them cancel each other out—that's forgiveness. And then, once we forgive each other, there's little left of what happened (in itself it didn't amount to much anyway); we may as well forget, too. We can act as if it never happened— that's a way after all in which it might never have happened."

But Jane objected one time more. "I agree with what you say about forgiveness, since even if you were wrong (I still think you were), it doesn't make much difference now. Your intentions were good, as I believe mine were; we've talked about what happened, and no great harm came of it anyway. Surely, then, we would do well to forgive each other. But it's not possible or even right simply to forget. Shouldn't we re- member how our disagreement came up, what we found fault with each other about? That way, the next time something like this begins to happen, we can avoid it. Experience keeps a dear school, after all—but then, we should learn from it, shouldn't we? And anyway, it's no good pretending that for- getting is voluntary. The surest way to remember is to try not to; you know that as well as I do. With forgiving or without it, memory holds on — so let's agree: we forgive, but not forget."

But have they not omitted something, this John and Jane, always so thoughtful, so prudently reasoned, so amiable towards each other? Only, I would argue, the most sure-footed of all the possible combinations, one that might surface twenty years later in a muted form so delicately turned that the most devoted connoisseur of the psyche's art could easily fail to recognize it. I speak here of the possibility that they — John, or Jane, or together — would indeed forget, put the history of their ideas aside, out of sight, but then discover that something else had lingered on. To forget, that is, but not to forgive.

A Bargain

"As many as you may slay, you will not kill your successor," Seneca the Stoic predicted to the murderous Nero, and soon afterward, at Nero's command, committed suicide. The turn of this phrase is itself brief but permanent. It is meant for the many of us—killers or not—who make bargains with the future, asking (we say) only for the reprieve of a moment, but thinking, in fact, for all time.

With the perfect faith of children, we believe that if we can defer, bargain for the grace of enough single moments, the texture of the whole will weaken, lose its compulsion, unravel just enough to let us—that is, the one of us, the "I"—slip through. We prefer this complicated misalliance to the simpler truth that there exists even now a future from which we are absent.

Filial Impiety

"Every craftsman loves the work of his own hands more than he would be loved by it, if it were to come to life." So the asceticism and humility of Aristotle show through the profusion of his thinking, his unwillingness to call anything in the whole of nature alien to him. A creator wills his own existence in what he creates; it is no wonder then that what he creates could never, even with life of its own to spend and with a large and generous sense of indebtedness, match that will.

The wisdom here is exemplary and chilling. For if Michelangelo's ardor could never have been requited for the Sistine Chapel, nor Mozart's spirit by *Don Giovanni*, the very spirit of the lover come to life; if Flaubert's passion for Mme. Bovary was never to be returned, no matter what words he, her creator, forced her to utter (was it this iniquity, we ask, that led him, dying, to curse her willingness to survive him?) — Why should we others feel slighted when we encounter the same evidence in the one test to which most of us, artists or not, are put? We shall love them anyway, after all — since they are, undeniably, our children.

Sameness and Difference

The lines are drawn around anti-Semitism in strong and fixed contours, without nuance, with little room left to doubt what they are pointing at: the Jew, the anti-Semite, the bystander who soon discovers that even in this role there is no innocence. But it is a mistake to conclude from such constancy that the imagination is not at work here, that the sameness in many dispersed acts of violation has been only imitative, banal, predictable. The imagination, it seems, needs only a bit of matter, the slightest friction, to begin to secrete the layers of its pearl. All that it requires is an occasion, *any* occasion, including, we have to admit, those of evil as well as good; it is not only moral light that warms the imagination.

So, consider the list of the twenty-two restrictions imposed on the Jews in Hamadan, Persia, 1892. Most of the rules are conventional, borrowed, perhaps not very interesting even in their first appearance — expressions of mere spite or nastiness. Thus, Regulation 6: "Jews are required to wear a badge of red cloth." Or, Regulation 7: "Jews are forbidden to build houses taller than those of a Muslim neighbor." Regulation 16: "The Jew cannot put on his coat. He must carry it rolled under his arm." But one item in the series shows an understanding of culture and personality that draws on almost untouched reaches of the spirit, areas that the inventiveness of modern social science hardly approaches in its will to anticipate the extent of human action. So, Regulation 5: "Jews are forbidden to wear matching shoes."

The reader with a practical turn of mind could understand this rule as only another, ironical form of taxation: the Jew must buy two pairs of shoes in order to have even one; or, conversely, as a joke in excesses, the Jew cannot have one pair of shoes without having two. But the impulse of the imagination is always more than utilitarian—and so here, too, with its proposals to violate the familiar order. Why should it be, we hear the unspoken question, that pairs are always similar, symmetrical, like? We know this custom immediately in our own clothing: gloves, socks, sleeves, trouser legs. And even there, of course, we are imitating nature itself, which is the most persistent spokesman for likeness, the inventor of the pair: hands, legs, cheeks, eyes, eyebrows, breasts. To see the one of any of these is to predict the other—a constancy that does not trouble even the strongest admirers of difference and originality. Even where there are more than pairs (toes, fingers, teeth), we recognize still the control of symmetry, a subordination to the principle of analogy. Nature itself thus seems committed to an economy of repetition. Burdened by the pressure always to invent, to make its own way, it understandably craves familiarity, regularity, the comfort of order, a promise of justice or equity.

Only the freak, the grotesque, can disrupt that order—and the Muslim clergy of Hamadan who set the fifth regulation prove that also man can will and create the incongruous, discover the means and indignities of lopsidedness. They might, those vendors of religious artfulness, had they been more consistent in their logic, have decreed that the mismatched shoes should also be forbidden to walk together. (That rule, too, would later be imposed on the Jews, but with little art, presented directly as cruelty). Perhaps only the clear rationality of a child could heal such violations—not, surely, by avenging, but by absorbing them. I once asked a young boy how it happened that one sock he was wearing was white and the other one brown. "Oh, that's the way they are," he reassured me; "I have another pair at home just like it."

The Seeds of History

❦

Because of the ages and distances they have to traverse, historical narratives leave little room for nuance or qualification — and so readers have learned to make allowance for the gaps in these records, for their unruly edges of generalization. Indeed, we have become so accustomed to give history the benefit of these doubts that error and even harsh injustice occasionally slip in under the same cover. To some of these lapses, repetition and tradition subsequently add their weight — and then what originated in a moment's inattention becomes a full-grown travesty: no one questions, no one doubts.

I am not thinking here of world-shaking events like the expulsion from Eden or the fall of more commonplace empires or even the inventive varieties and fortunes of war. These are, after all, so extensive in detail that no single set of eyes could possibly hold them in view; thus, partiality and revision are inevitable in their histories. I have in mind rather the simpler images of individual figures, famed in themselves and drawing on famous genealogies, whom we have come to assume as familiars, tried and supposedly true. Yet it is also among these common figures of discourse that we find some who are traduced virtually every time they are named — perhaps not out of malice but with a presumption that in the end is no less wounding, since it is our sense of history as a whole that is the victim.

Consider, for one example, the tragic Oedipus — recalled now by many who know nothing of Greek legend or the writing of Sophocles but who immediately recognize the "complex" that has come to attach his name to every male child (that is, to every male). What thus remains of Oedipus's repeated and inventive efforts to escape the destiny predicted for him is only one and a much simpler impulse: the passion that drove him toward his own mother — a passion so urgent as to cause him to vie for her love with every possible rival, beginning first (naturally) with his own father, his nearest and dearest competitor. So fiercely ridden was the bearer of this desire that he would commit murder in its behalf — symbolically if that had sufficed, but in fact (perhaps even by preference) literally.

Yet, quite differently and on the other side, there is Oedipus, the king himself, raging *against* the fate predicted for him as no other son has done since. Admittedly, he would later declare — sorrowfully, but also, it has to be said, boastfully — that "No living man has loved as I have." But even these vainglorious words were meant for a queen who was unimaginable to him — actual but unimaginable — as his mother. He came to her, we know, in full flight away from her, searching for any avenue of escape that great energy and awful fear might discover. Was there anything Oedipus could have done that he did not do to prove that the Oedipus complex was not his — that *he* at least was free of it? Even those most fully persuaded of psychology's depths do not deny the conscience of Oedipus's efforts. (They sometimes assert that he knowingly chose to defeat his own purpose — but against such claims no evidence would suffice.) Yet he is remembered now, travestied, in the complex that finds him struggling not to escape but to win his mother in love, murdering his father on the way: he, Oedipus, who in order to avoid the history so ascribed to him did everything except blot out the very light of day—and then, discovering what he had done against desire, extinguished the light of day as well.

Perhaps something in the envied majesty of the classical Greeks—or is it only in Freud's arranged marriage of history and instinct?—nourishes such willful injustice. For if we move sidewards, one short step, to Narcissus, we find also there the pattern of travesty—there, in the narcissist, so self-absorbed, so enchanted by his (or her) own beauty that no rival would be admitted. In the eyes and heart of the narcissist, love requires—allows—only one party, the one closest at hand (or face), the single I who both looks and is seen. There is no other, not because love is blind but because love sees so clearly; familiarity becomes the only intimacy.

And yet Narcissus himself? Looking at his reflection in the water—the one mirror he knew, thus ignorant of it *as* a mirror—Narcissus falls in love. That he was beautiful we may believe; that he fell in love with *himself*: what evidence is there of that? His reflection revealed to him the existence of someone else in the world with such powers of enchantment that Narcissus, from that one wordless appearance, could afterwards conceive no other love.

Was it himself, then, that he desired so intensely as to hold death the one alternative to fulfillment? A mischievous question, since it is uncertain that Narcissus—knowing nothing of mirrors or reflections—could even *conceive* of the self that was his own. But from having walked in the world, he surely knew well and fully about others. And no less surely, then, it was from the longing for one such other that he died, for someone else without whom, he proved, he could not live. There are, we know, people who sacrifice themselves so that loved companions or children may survive. And we know also of people who, loving others in vain, have died only because of that denial. But the numbers in both these groups are small, with the second still smaller than the first. And the figure among these whom we know best is Narcissus himself.

But then how does the defamation suffered by Oedipus and Narcissus occur? Perhaps what happens here is that first a story is invented and only then is a person or name found to whom it is fitted—rather than the other (historical) way round. This indeed seems to provide the only possible understanding of how Onan became the onanist: Onan, who, we find in the biblical source, had nothing farther from his mind than the solitary half-pleasure of masturbation; who wished only to avoid having a son through coercion, taking the place of his dead elder brother in the bed of his sister-in-law. We know nothing in particular of Tamar herself except that she wished for a son of her own as ardently as Onan wished for one of his. And this too we understand: it was through the first son that the line carried—through the eldest son's family if there were sons; through Onan, the next in line, if there were none. The issue, then, concerned property and inheritance, not sex. And in that early but heartfelt bourgeois world, was it so unreasonable that Onan, driven against his own interest to copulate, would try to save what he could of himself by spilling his seed on the ground?

That God struck Onan dead for this act gave Onan no opportunity to demonstrate that the act itself had no attraction for him. Still less did he have the chance to disprove a suspicion of masturbation's habit. (It is clear, in fact, that Onan could not have been an onanist before that, since then God's punishment would also have reached him earlier.) Artfully, we use the Latin now—coitus interruptus—for the act that Onan did perform; and indeed in certain orthodoxies there is sin in that as well (although in a Bible filled with violations for which the death penalty is mandated, birth control does not otherwise bear that judgment).

And again, of course, however coitus interruptus is judged, Onan's name has since been identified not with that but with a different act altogether: different means, different ends, different pleasure. Onanism, in the misdemeanor now unjustly charged to Onan, has nothing to do with birth or its prevention; it does not require a third or even a second party. Indeed it is best known for its solitariness, the act of one hand. Thus we may wonder here, as sharply as anywhere else, how such misrepresentation could occur; even travesties, one supposes, must retain something of their historical grounds.

The one explanation of how two such different acts could be conflated — and Onan traduced — depends, I believe, on a view of those acts from the unlikely standpoint of Onan's seed itself. That, at least, comes to a single and common end in both versions of onanism, the original and the travesty together. But this explanation, it will be evident, is far from a justification. With so many eminent agents open to judgment here — man, woman, God — and with the morality of history itself at stake: Does it seem quite fair to give Onan's seed the last and deciding word?

Paid in Full

✿

Kierkegaard writes that "In the realm of the spirit, there is absolute justice," and there are two ways of understanding this brief lesson in moral geography; both of them mark a place for virtue, but one of them is profound, the other merely accessible. The readier meaning calls our attention to consequences: a person acts—and then, later, the consequences of that act come home to him, righting imbalance, rewarding him, perhaps, or exacting a price. This seems an efficient doctrine, stern, certainly sufficient with its appeal to an all-knowing history to stir the impulse for morality. That it makes justice a matter of prudence, deferring to a system of practical checks and balances, hardly impedes its work. Everyone, we understand, eventually faces the consequences of his actions, even if the actions are not publicly known, even if they are not recognized by the agent himself. There is the compression here that one expects in any reconstruction of history, the adherence of action to effect that surely encourages conviction. Dante's Inferno is the densest assembly of those who experience this elegant symmetry—the murderers condemned to spend eternity trying to keep afloat in blood; the false prophets with their heads twisted backwards, never again to see anything in front of them. Had they *then* been given the choice, they would surely have acted otherwise.

And yet, and yet: even the compression in this account leaves a gap that might carry with it a possibility of deliverance, remission. For if the consequences of actions can be balanced, traded off, there may in the course of a lifetime be enough space between the action and the consequence to insert still *other* actions—that is, to mitigate, to forestall, even to change direction.

But not, it seems, to find justice. Only consider the alternative, and the difference is clear. Let the action itself be the mark made, the imprint—deed and quality together. To this, other marks may be added later, but they do not supersede the early ones. There is in the spirit no surface for erasure; everything counts, just as it is; no one moment displaces another. Actions, whether for good or evil, then, do not *leave* a mark (implying a distance); they *are* the mark. The condensation is complete: judgments passed on them are only the facts themselves.

Looking outward, we sometimes pretend to ourselves that we may see our actions as we choose to—by looking to the rhetoric of history, examining ourselves in shaded mirrors, or by the response of others to us. But Kierkegaard dispels these myths of distance: the mark we make also affects what we look with or by (even when we are not looking). We do not escape it by closing our eyes, not by living underground, not even, in this harsh continuum, by radically changing the self that has acted, since the change as well as the self will then be noted. What could come closer to true equity than that we should be exactly what we do—not more, not less.

Circles and Lines

We often acknowledge Nietzsche's passion and wit, his restless and knowing eye for imposture, his assassination of moral
conceits. Because of the skepticism that stands behind all of
these, perhaps because we cannot stop distrusting irony, we
do not easily credit Nietzsche himself with moral genius; we
would be unlikely, in any event, to look for evidence of it in
his doctrine of the "eternal recurrence": his odd, mythlike suggestion that, whatever the moment or situation that engages
us—banal or decisive, sipping a cup of coffee, declaring or
denying or betraying love—we shall many times again find
ourselves repeating the same scene, uttering the same words,
rehearsing the same expectations. But this idea is intended to
scotch the usual turns of moral satisfaction; it is in fact itself
an ethical imperative. In it we see why the circle rather than
the line is the perfect figure—and how geometry, the reckon-
ing of mere space, turns out, as the Pythagoreans had promised, to be a moral science after all.

Imagine a stage-set for this drama, with the aged Kant
seated in an armchair at one corner of the stage—weak, failing, a few days, in fact, before his death. He struggles to rise
in order to greet a visitor who pleads with him not to trouble

himself: "I have not yet lost my sense of humanity," Kant replies, pulling himself up—and we see in his slight movement the vast extent of the categorical imperative: In a single action, in *any* single action, we choose not only for ourselves, but for everyone. We would not, we could not, hope to derive the expanse of moral reason from mere inclination or the occasional feeling.

A burden, we can well admit: a person starts simply, choosing an action that at the moment seems right. But he may not, even for one moment, forget the bonds that tie it and him to others, that weave the moral fabric he wears. Brothers, we say, not just under the skin but in it. What could be a more faithful or ardent guide?

And Nietzsche, whistling his way onstage, has an answer: the song of eternal recurrence, to be sung in many—countless—refrains. For the power of Kant's categorical imperative is horizontal, impersonal: in choosing for oneself, one chooses for others. You must—here the ideal—*forget* yourself, your own needs, wants, future. And this, however, burdensome, still has an ease about it. Not only because any single act immediately finds itself, and then its agents, the member of a community (could the first motive for the categorical imperative have been simple loneliness?), but because the community, after all, is rich in possibility—so laden with alternatives, so short in memory, that any single act may well be diluted there, put aside. Certainly we, the individual agents, have buffers of forgetfulness that we readily apply when once an act is over and done. Shame itself has a limited claim: linked to a fading memory, it gradually loses the power to make us squirm, to compel others to expose us, to breed resentment. But what, Nietzsche asks his audience, if this—any—action of yours were universalized not for others, but for you yourself? If, just as you did it once, you must also find yourself doing it again—and then, again and again? For Nietzsche, it is not a maxim for all other people that one proposes, but a maxim for oneself in all time. As though for each of our actions—however separated, however discreet—we can hardly detect a future moment when we are *not* doing it.

"A sobering thought," Nietzsche concludes, drunk with himself and the prospect of a long future. Kant, struggling to his feet again, this time to bid his guest farewell, manages to stand up, but cannot find anything more to say. Even the words he had used before escape him now.

and People

The Price of a Possible World
🕮

Leibniz, invoking the principles of plenitude and God's power, asserts the (possible) existence of an infinite number of possible worlds—and the actual existence, because of God's goodness, of the best of them. It is hard not to sympathize with the impulse here, since if there is order, it must rule over what is not as well as over what is; actuality, it might be argued, is only a special case of the possible. Thus, that the best of all possible worlds *ought to* exist, whether by God's choice or by the selection of nature, makes sense—although, admittedly, the claim itself seems tinged with wistfulness, a reluctant and sad doubt.

So the resentments against Leibniz's assurance, the taunts against his confidence in the world, are not so much unreasonable as bad tempered, captious. Surely, nobody with Leibniz's history of broken promises (his own and those of others), of interrupted or unwritten writings, continually struggling either for or with patrons, could easily mistake the recalcitrant and uneven texture of the world. Pangloss was pleased with the world because he was pleased with himself; Leibniz founded a world on reason that clashed sharply, disharmoniously, with his own experience.

131

Perhaps it is for this reason—it is impossible, of course, to be certain—that a significant omission occurs in the otherwise coherent (it is not too strong to say, circular) plan of his work. Admittedly, if we ask *where are* those possible worlds that, because they were not the best one, never became actual—we ask unfairly, a breach of metaphysical etiquette: "Where?" is not more a question for possibilities than it is for spirits or numbers. But still, those possible worlds were real possibilities—and here we find ourselves troubled in a way that Leibniz himself perhaps intended: a last and bitter joke by the man on whom others would batten for his supposedly heedless optimism. The people and events in those only possible worlds, those that never came into existence, and the lives, conversations, colors, hatreds, sunsets that populate them: Do we know enough to be certain that we are not among them?

Notice that not a word of Leibniz's work must be altered to allow this question; indeed, there is nothing to forestall it. What, in fact, would be more likely for the one flaw in a slightly less than perfect world than that its inhabitants should mistakenly believe that theirs, with that single flaw, was indeed the perfect one? The inhabitants could hardly be faulted for making this mistake; they would have had no experience of an actual world with which to compare it.

Endings

History is judgment, and Michelangelo would hardly have quarreled with its verdict: even in his lifetime, the celebrations had begun. But then, too, a certain irony, an edge of reserve that found him shadowed by a peculiar incontinence — not the common incontinence of starting irregularly, without restraints, but a finer, subtler one of never finishing what he had begun. There was never a question, from his earliest years, about the artist's power — but that energy seemed always to battle against containment, against the limits that creation itself required. Why would he not complete what he had bargained for, been paid to do, what he himself had undertaken? The dunning letters from his sponsors could later have been directed to a hapless debtor in the pages of Dickens, to a schlemiel in Kasrilevka. The artist himself did not deny their justice. That he would not finish the works he had contracted for suggested to him as well only weakness, a lack of resolve.

But like the rest of us, history, taxing Michelangelo with this debt, may be mistaking its own form for reality. It thinks of endings as it thinks of beginnings — that they occur only as consciousness dictates, only through knowledge and conviction. But what if endings do not follow such formality, so easy an appeal to calculation? Why not say, more simply, that the end is where the work stops? We look now at Michelangelo's slaves, frozen in their struggle to get out of the marble. Had they escaped, had Michelangelo their jailer given them leave, surely our view would be different: we would never know that the slaves had struggled at all. And it would not then be an ending to the same work that we knew, but, with the different ending, a different work.

We realize this still more urgently in recognizing that even when a struggle is over, it remains still a struggle. And why then require more of those slaves than we do of ourselves? Let the completion, the ending, be in the supposed middle—a surprise perhaps to Michelangelo himself. The eye (his, ours) would quickly adjust—and who among us would be unwilling to admit that Michelangelo's hands might have known more than his head?

Memory Now

No one, having once read it, will misplace Nietzsche's allusion to forgetting as a creative act. What a remarkable contribution to plenitude, we could well say, speaking from a world more used to loss and diminution: friends, places. Forgetting: what seems on the face of it mere absence, a confession of finitude, the hedging of experience by individual withdrawals—turns out instead to be an instrument by which man expands, adds to himself, *literally* adds to himself.

For we are, once we concede to forgetting as many and various motives as remembering, two persons. The one: narrow, selective, known to us, consciously chosen within the bounds of a pattern. The second is larger, more diverse, richer: everything we have seen or felt, but which, then, we have decided to put aside. Undoubtedly this second-person "I" is so large—only think of the ground that he covers—that we try to comfort ourselves with the thought that he is less real than the first-person "I" whom we know and cherish. But there the second one also is, beside us always, massive, more ourselves—counting by bulk alone—than the first. To be sure, we may well have forgotten exactly what he says, his associations, the fabric of his imagery—but we cannot deny either that we once knew these, that we have chosen to exclude them: we thus give them, *him*, a cut direct that we would hesitate to do with any figure who spoke directly to us.

It is quite understandable that we should balk at lending this other person our own name. But the jealousy of possession also represents fear, as the commitments of a present are threatened, as the memories we have consciously kept by us are denied. There are many good reasons, then, for wanting to preserve the distance between these two selves, but we realize too that curiosity alone may at some time lead us to strike up an acquaintance quite openly. The formal introduction would be awkward but not difficult to predict: "Self," we say, "meet Other—Other, Self." There will, of course, be a question of protocol here. It cannot be easy to decide who should be named first.

Class Struggle

We know little of how ideas are born, and it is probably because of this that we are so ready to attach the names of people to them, to think of concepts as children. Certainly we are more comfortable with people — and by giving their names to ideas, we suggest the ties of genealogy, a texture of history, the aura of beginnings and also of ends for ideas that otherwise seem cold, independent, larger than life. So, there are Plato's Forms and Darwin's Evolution, Descartes's Cogito, Copernicus's Revolution. The fit here is not always even, and the person attached is often only an abbreviation for the names of many others. Darwin did not himself speak of "evolution," it turns out — and others, before Copernicus, had moved the earth from its center.

About the Swede Linnaeus, however, no such quibbles are possible. The classification of nature, the ideal and practice of universal order and taxonomy are his, fully, cleanly — one is tempted to say that they are *him*. Not, of course, that he alone or for the first time sorted nature into categories; not even that the vision of natural plenitude, nature's fulsomeness, was only his — but that no one had brought these two together so urgently. Admittedly, this passion owes something to the ingenuity of the bourgeoisie. It is the ideal of comfort that rules here, where everyone has and knows his place; Marx himself was not to describe the compulsion for social order more dramatically. Certainly the cardinal sin, the original sin, for Linnaeus's system is the idea of the exception, the freak, the breach in nature.

There is grandeur here, however, as well as economy, a sense of the sublime—for nothing is left out and what is included has identity but no limit. The sweep of vision relates and divides every organism in nature, living or dead; it leaves nothing over for a viewer who would detach himself from them to breathe with. The surest evidence for this claim of exhaustion we find in Linnaeus the man; for there, in his own person, was represented a second and conflicting theory that only two hundred years later received a name (one, as it happened, that was not his). I refer here to the puzzle identified by Bertrand Russell: Russell's Paradox—and Linnaeus's early version of the paradox, what lingers now as an uneasy epitaph to his life work: that the classifier of all classes did not find himself to be the member of a class.

Linnaeus never used this formulation; it is I who apply it, perhaps anachronistically. But there is hardly any alternative when we recall that the great and orderly Linnaeus, having served the world of conscience as a model, having given shape and reason to the extravagance of nature, having found for every other creature a place and a kind—should himself then have gone mad.

Risen

"Roll up your bedclothes on rising, and smooth out the imprint of your body," goes one of the rules of the Pythagoreans; and even if we have no more than those words themselves (we know only of the practice, not the explanation), we understand that housekeeping is not the issue here. But what then stands behind the words? That we must leave sleep intact when we enter the day? That as everything, in justice, requires its due, we have moral obligations also to beds?

Neither of these alternatives can be excluded; they do not even compete with each other. But the heart of the answer is clearly elsewhere, and what comes to mind here is the debt that Plato never quite repaid to Pythagoras. To be sure, Plato himself calls attention to the doctrine of numbers—that magical vision in which each quality or virtue is known as the member of an order. Numbers, the Pythagoreans see, those permanent and rational tokens, never fade in or out of existence— and from this constancy comes the ground they provide for moral virtues as well. Thus, justice is 4; marriage, 5; opportunity—for the Pythagoreans, this too is deliberate, a virtue—7. There could never be a pretext for subtracting from these qualities, indeed not even for adding to them.

We assume that Plato was a debtor here for his celebrated Theory of Forms—those unchanging models of justice and piety, of courage and the Good around which the philosopher, the lover of wisdom, circles. But Plato did not rest with these, and it has remained a mystery for later philosophers, writing the footnotes to Plato, why or when he stretched this doctrine to include in it the things of the world—beds, eyes, bodies: Forms to which he also offers the prize of reality and perfection. Thus it is no reactionary turn, not even a peculiar literal-mindedness that draws us back here to that first legacy of the Pythagoreans, the fear with which members of the cult started off each morning: that to leave one's Form in the bedclothes would mean having to walk about without it for the rest of the day.

This was not, I think, for them or for Plato, a fear of loneliness, a craving for the familiar companionship that one's shadow, for example, provides—but a passion for reality, specifically our own. As we rarely escape hoping to realize the self that we *really* are, the self that, beneath another surface, does not make mistakes, is keen and pure, so, in order to make it live, we give that self the only shape we ourselves can create—the impression of absence. Thus, too, when Plato extends the Forms to things and qualities in addition to people, we understand that he does this not out of generosity, certainly not in the spirit of democracy, but only to reinforce the claims of the one self, the "I," that needs all the reassurance it can get. Without the Form of that self, the Pythagoreans rightly guess, there would be no getting out of bed in the first place.

Borges as Borges

We try, after all, each of us, to make the world better. At least we would fashion it in our own image—and that, for most of us, is a promise of good. Borges the writer lived in a world of books; they held few possibilities that he himself did not know or foresee. He imagines, at one moment, that every possible book had been written; we have assurance, then, that it would be no less difficult to find a book in the complete library of books than it would be to write it. Or he mentions the village librarian, constrained by a small budget, who reads the reviews of books and then, conscientiously, himself writes the books for his library shelves.

In all this, Borges does not question the books themselves. They are, as are his own—we suppose him thinking— real enough. And there is a point here, surely, for quarrel. Is there in each person a nature that admits no end for the making of books? Or is it perhaps itself a story—this endless profusion of printed pages, a manner of reassurance by the fact of their own fiction that fiction at least is real?

I have an idea of this that might ease this unending challenge, shrug off the burden of that printed mirror of reality that condemns us either to search constantly for new reading or to find escape from reading by becoming writers ourselves. Is it so improbable that the many appearances of the printed word — the stories, the novels, the poems — are, beneath their surfaces, the work of a single author? One, to be sure, of great energy, of demotic character — a roving nature that leads him from an evening's sitting of lyric poetry in an English countryside to another day's epic on the fall of Greek empire. He has friends, this writer, and no vainglory himself. Or perhaps so much more than anyone else that he can act in all humility towards them. So he signs his friends' names to his writings — and other names to the reviews or criticism of those works, which he also writes. He is truly a shaker of the world, this writer, but compelled more than ambitious. He writes as birds sing — not because he wants to, but because he does not know how not to. He is not even very happy with most of the fictions he creates or with the lies he has felt obliged to tell about their origins; deceit does not come easily to him in his other affairs.

I doubt, incidentally, that this writer's name could have been Borges. The author who went under the name of Borges could hardly have written other than he did.

One Out of Many

🦂

Viewed from one direction, making a decision seems the simplest act possible. To decide to do something need not move us out of our chairs; we do not require anyone else's collaboration, we do not need tools or technology, we are not obliged to write the decision down or to say it aloud. All that we need is the deciding itself, and this is only a matter of making up our minds, which are, after all, always ours to make up. There is no waiting in line here, no asking permission, no deferral to rank. Pleading or cajoling may at times quicken the response, but only after the mind that is cajoled or pleaded with agrees — an independence that contrasts sharply with our powerlessness in the physical world. The laws of physics or chemistry, history's irreversibility, the canny inscriptions of the genetic code: we may haggle and carp, we may try brute force — but in the end they remain always beyond our range. I cannot "make up" my body, but I can always make up my mind.

And yet, simple as the process should be, it is rarely straightforward. For one thing, the alternatives I have to choose between are only possibilities: I have in hand only the imagined touch of what, at some later time, may be present in fact. And even after I push my way past this vague cushion of possibility, the road beyond is cluttered with obstacles: having determined the choice I prefer, I still have to decide whether — and why — to act on it.

Most of us have heard the story that there is no space between these two stages — decision and act; that even in theory and certainly in practice, to have one is also to have the other. No doubt there is a certain truth in this; so, for example, to decide and then not to act is also to have decided not to act. But if you take it as a general rule, you will know little about the way the mind works. Why, after all, should we who decide then absent ourselves — something we are almost always *forced* to do in other actions? *There* goes the hand (or the mouth or the leg), moving quickly along — and in such moments, the mind agrees to stand aside, watching what happens like the spectator at a show. It is not unreasonable, then, that when it comes to deciding, the mind would choose always to be present, to surface in midcourse for corrections or revision. Thus, even decisions that are unified and swift, entirely of a piece, turn out in fact to be plural and divided: always there are parts to them, and then also parts of the parts.

However we judge it, then, there is no pathology in Kafka's account of the way *he* made decisions, although it contrasts sharply with more common accounts: "If I want to turn right," he wrote, "I first turn left, then sadly edge rightwards." What is unusual here is mainly that Kafka was willing to disclose this closely held secret; our debt to him, then, is as much to his candor as to his eyesight. In the view most of us have of our decisions, the turn to the left and the edging rightwards are compressed into one. Rather than admit the hindrance of conscience, we represent any decision we make as a single motion. Thus it is the combination of Kafka's sharp eye and quick courage that forces us to recognize in what seems smooth unity a number of parts and stages, including the one that first sets everything in motion by going in the contrary direction

When Kafka described the last step in his decision as "sad," he was no doubt regretting that the motion itself ever came to an end — not that he wished to shorten the decision, or that he was willing to give up the freedom that so lengthened it. This in itself distinguishes Kafka from those of us who would willingly exchange the freedom to move in the contrary direction for the power to move directly and quickly, as in a single motion. (The upshot of this will for unity is that by it we move more quickly but often in the contrary direction anyway). We cannot explain this difference between Kafka and ourselves as only a difference in eyesight, although many literary oculists who disagree on other matters have indeed reached the conclusion that Kafka's eyesight was extraordinary: he could see close-up and as large as life what other viewers observe only at a distance or, more often, not at all.

Fables Refabled

❦

There was once a fox who was both clever and single-minded, and who had a special fondness for grapes. Trotting through the forest one day, he spotted an unusually lush vine that was caught in the branches of several trees and dangled there, just beyond his reach. The fox leaped at the grapes a few times without much hope, and then settled down to some serious training. He dieted carefully and jogged around the forest religiously, practicing especially the running jump. At the end of a week, he still was missing the grapes by a half-foot, at the end of a month by four inches. After two months, just when his family and friends were beginning to find his running around tiresome and his single-mindedness a bore, he made a spectacular lunge and pulled the vine down to earth. Himself also — for as he gobbled them, he had to admit that the grapes that were lush and beautiful to look at were terribly sour to the taste. He could not hide this disappointment from his assembled family and friends, but he put a brave face on it by saying that after all he had enjoyed the running and jumping, and in fact had never felt more fit in his life.

Ever since that time, we speak of people who claim that virtue is its own reward as sour grapes.

* * * * * * * *

There was once a shepherd boy who because there were no fire alarms to pull in his part of the fields thought it was very clever to shout "Wolf! Wolf!" and then stand and watch the people from the village tumble out to help him. He was, aside from this, a nice boy and a good shepherd, and the villagers didn't mind too much when he fooled them three or four times. But many times later, when it became clear that the shepherd would not be content with moderation, the villagers told him that they weren't going to come out to the fields anymore when he yelled "Wolf! Wolf!"

The very next day, a wolf showed up in the pasture and the boy knew that he would have to shout much louder than he had before in order to get the villagers to come out to help him. So he did, with shrieks that had an unearthly echo—and two things happened. The villagers never showed up, because although they noticed the difference in his shouts, they thought that it proved how right they were to teach him a lesson. And second, the wolf was so frightened by the noise coming from a creature he wasn't especially interested in that he ran off.

Ever since that time, we speak of someone who beats the moralists without giving up his own game as the boy who cried wolf.

Taking the Cure

Jacques Derrida—may he live till 120—will probably, even with the best of luck, have to see a doctor during that time. The doctor may then decide, after examining him, that some medication is indicated; thus he writes out a prescription. To whom does Derrida take this brief but original text? To those who have learned to read from him? the poststructuralists? the metahistorians? It is unlikely; one could in fact forgive Derrida an unspoken hope that the traditional curriculum had not yet been revised in schools of pharmacy. Thus he is reassured when, on entering a shop marked by the sign of Aesculapius, he notices the white-coated technologist patiently standing behind the counter. Derrida hands him the physician's note and waits expectantly. The pharmacist pores over the note with grave concentration and then moves out of sight, behind a second and higher counter. After a short time, he comes back into view and places on the lower counter between them a small vial. It is in fact the smallest vial that Derrida has ever seen; surprise and puzzlement show clearly in his face as he reaches for his wallet. As he fumbles with this, the unspoken question is communicated—and the response also makes its way: "But, *cher maître*," the pharmacist pleads, troubled, knowingly, warmly, "I assure you that I have done my very best. You of all people will understand, however, that all I can provide you with, on the basis of what the doctor wrote, is a trace."

Objections to Objects

The modern world saunters between two poles, named in their common menace the "subjective" and the "objective." The conflict here has been strenuous, not often polite. On the one hand, the ideals of detachment, disinterest, searching truth out for its own sake—*the* truth that like an unknown continent waits for discovery by those who deserve it, who by asceticism, leaving behind their lives, properties, interests, have earned its favors. The other side prides itself on body and impulse—the lack of purity. Not for it the transparency of ideas when the richness of flesh is available. So the head is sacrificed to the limbs, feeling is celebrated, and language itself is produced by touch. No mind without a skin, this second view starts out, moderately enough; it ends with the mind all skin—a conclusion that warms the defender of objective truth to his passion: "Irrationalist," he calls, summoning the loudest curse he can imagine, "where would we be if science depended on you? Who would build the airplanes? Who would cut out the cancers?"

It is difficult for anyone who loves books, those compact markers of an orderly and detachable reason, not to sympathize with the cool reflection of objectivity that asks no more than soberly to put passion in its proper place, to give it—like anything else—its due. And so I did and perhaps would yet, until I came across the remains of the British general, Sir Douglas Haig—commander-in-chief of the British forces in the Great War and of the mud bogs of Flanders, Verdun, Ypres (Wipers, his soldiers' rendering of this was—often a gasped last word, to the end humanizing the alien); responsible for the deaths, in the round figures that historians use for currency when no one is likely to quibble about hundreds or even thousands, of hundreds of thousands. General Haig, we hear, stern, efficient, a figure of authority, made disinterest a policy in his judgment of strategy and tactics—a moral principle of objectivity that he judged was necessary in order to fight the war. He would not, he said, follow the commanderly ritual of visiting in hospitals the wounded soldiers who served under him. Obliged to give the orders to send still other men into battle, he must keep his vision unimpaired.

Here, certainly, the killing question becomes inevitable. What—in the search for sanctity: clean hands, pure heart; in the pursuit of disinterest, detachment, impersonality; in paring away the body so that the object of its design appears untainted, unalloyed—what would Haig have left to see with?

Repairs

Gödel's Axiom of Incompleteness formalizes what experience sooner or later tells us all: that whatever seems whole, full, even the most convincingly seamless fabric, contains within itself the germ of disintegration—that there are no complete systems, none that allow even the most devout acolyte to rest inside them. Perfection, then, the very idea of completeness or totality, is a fiction—an understandable effort to find coherence for ourselves, in ourselves, but a fiction nonetheless.

I knew someone once who, grown to disillusion through the discovery that what is bright and promising in a young man (himself) becomes dead weight within a few short years, undertook, as a way of settling accounts, to communicate this constant and inevitable feature of incompleteness to the world. A moral imperfectionist, one resilient acquaintance called him—although for himself and with an air of modesty, the Incompleteness Man claimed that he acted as a matter of principle, in the interest of leading others to the goal of self-knowledge. So he went about demonstrating for every system of ideas where the gap was; for every account, its flaw and then its demise. He was feared, of course, this critic, because he had consistency on his side and also a sharp and clever eye: no statement that paused for breath was immune to his energies. Even when others would put the broken places together again or add to them new ones, the aura of his criticism remained.

He himself, of course, could not be happy in this role; to one of a collection of very beautiful girlfriends (each of them ignorant of the existent of the others), he once confided, without a trace of irony, "I feel that my life is incomplete."

The woman who told me about this confession mistook it for an offer of marriage; that was the point of the story, in fact, as she related it to me. And if you ask me how I, who did not actually hear the conversation, could know that the Incompleteness Man spoke then without irony, I say only two things. First, that in the many conversations I have had with him, I have never heard him speak other than literally. Second, that irony assumes at least the possibility of completeness, of satisfaction.

Particles and Fields: A Lament

In respect to feelings and the life of the spirit as well as in physics there is disagreement between the field theory and the particle theory. On the particle theory of feeling, experience accumulates, piece by piece, one placed on another, forming composites or chains that move sideways or even turn backwards—but always with anything added in the present distinct from what accrued in the past. As new moments or nuances appear, the older ones remain at least what they were; they do not—*could* not—diminish. The past then affords only another view of what was once present, and there is comfort to be found here in repetition and reliability: the world, at least, is always with us.

And then there is the field theory in which each moment spreads through the whole; the center is everywhere at once, and what happens at one point in the present affects all others, in the past and the future as well as now. It is an unlikely conception of feelings, this—that we cannot judge or have them piecemeal, that the past no less than the future is always open to revision. So, on this account, we may find ourselves displaced in the past even after having (we thought) put it behind us. And indeed, this much I have myself learned from experience, after resisting it constantly (so much as to be unaware of the resistance) — in the death of my dear uncle. For at that moment, I discovered that it was not only this one piece of a world that slipped away; all that I had known or felt in the past and then after it, in the future, was altered, tinged by a loss that made its presence constantly known, even in moments that were otherwise full and welcome.

The discovery of this loss, I have to admit, was accompanied by gain. For through it I now recognize that what had before seemed fixed and neutral in the past, straightforward matters of fact, had all along held an unknown sweetness; the later loss that retroactively took value away from everything that existed earlier proved that the value had been present. The gain here, moreover, was larger than the person: there was, I learned, goodness in the world; so the new absence of this one part testified. So, too, in death, my uncle had given to me as he always had — without expecting that I give anything in return. There was the gift itself, and there was the world to which, in each part, it had been added, and there was then later, finally, the constant testimony of its loss.

3½ on Death

⚙

1. Talmon knew he was about to die, and others knew this as well. His doctor, a young man of old self-confidence, had told Talmon that the growth he had first discovered by manipulation was malignant and that it had spread into the organs. But secrets also have faces, and although Talmon continued with his work at the Institute of Physics, his colleagues—he saw in their faces—discovered what he had learned. Is there no privacy? Talmon asked himself, and then, more precisely: Is it not enough that my outside is outside? Must my inside also be outside?

Talmon had planned for death, it seemed to him, all the days of his life. As a schoolboy of fifteen, a pain had struck him sharply in the side after a long bicycle ride in the country summer. The connection came to him by what he later called his mortal intuition. This is my death, he said to himself, with the smell of the birch trees baked by the sun still fresh in his nostrils. And he spent long hours after that, giving himself to the symbol. I shall never see my twentieth year, he lectured himself portentously, and went back to his study of geometry. There, where parallel lines meet, I will be that day, and Euclid could find no more sober fool.

He had, of course, passed the age of twenty. He took a good degree in physics—charting the movement of certain subatomic particles—and as a graduate student, he wrote a number of papers joining those movements to the properties of the nuclei of living cells. These papers were speculative, but the images they outlined soon began to appear in the writing of other biophysicists. What had started for Talmon as autobiography became in the hands of others a science—and recognition came to him as a founder, a man of "large scientific imagination" as Lonham, the Cambridge Nobelist, described him at the dinner honoring Talmon's sixtieth birthday.

The visit to the young doctor followed soon after this celebration, and a short operation after that. (Talmon knew by looking at the clock that there was nothing to be done for him.) And now he waited, sitting in the office attached to his laboratory and writing up the notes of his latest experiment. The late Talmon working on his latest experiment, he muttered to himself. Why not the latest Talmon?

One thought now, as Talmon reviewed his future, persisted. Yes, he said to himself, I fear both the dying and the death. But the one only for the other. Pain, after all, is tolerable as long as one tolerates it. But why is the end of it so fearful? He tried to conceive of experiments by which he could determine the answer. After all, he argued with himself, we do not know what lies on the other side. And strictly speaking, for science, not to know is not to make inferences. Yet the anxiety is real. What does it conceal? What could remove it?

The day when Talmon discovered the answer to his question became his last day at the institute. He told the assistants in his laboratory that he was leaving early and left the papers on his desk as they were being worked on, most of them still unmarked. He called the director of the institute the next morning to request leave for several weeks to settle a "personal" matter. When the neighbors broke into his flat after a week's silence, they found Talmon sitting in his chair, dead, with a small bottle of pills in his hand. On the reading table next to him was a short note addressed to no one in particular.

> If I waited longer, I would be waiting for the whole world to die with me. Only so, I have discovered, would I face death with equanimity. It is too long to wait, of course, and some desires anyway are unworthy. Best regards.

Unsigned, as it was unaddressed. And for whom, the neighbors asked each other, were the regards intended?

* * * * * * * *

2. Nemerov was a composer of obituaries. Not by profession but by passion, and not from a desire to eulogize others but to mourn himself. Like other passions, this one flared and waned. But he was never without it, and the comfort it gave him, like the pain of obsession, was constant. As a businessman of prominence, he had seen his name in the newspapers many times. And no doubt, he said to himself, many more—except for one. Not that it wouldn't appear—but that he would not see it. Nemerov Dead—at 48 or 51 or 45, he filled out the headline, depending on how the day struck him; even at forty, he was ready to predict the syntax.

He tried to understand the times when he began composing. Was it when he wished he was in another business, or when he was tired? When he felt guilty for the crimes his wife charged him with? But there was no pattern. As he slammed the door of his car in the parking lot of his company, the empty space between him and the next car startled him: "Nemerov Falls into Place," the obituary would begin wryly, and would go on to tell how he had left home that Tuesday morning in good spirits and with no warning. No *visible* warning, Nemerov corrected the article. "Nemerov Dead on Vacation," the careless headline would say; casting the fly into a beaver pond, grown around with aspen trees, he caught a glimpse of the paper and the story. He saw it as clearly as the other obituaries that he did not write and that marched daily in firm lines along the last page of the local *Tribune*. "Nemerov Enjoys Final Hours at the Movies": He *watched* the words flash on the screen, just after the coming attractions—although his wife, buried in the darkness next to him, gave no signs of having noticed. "Nemerov's Last Supper." The words wrote themselves over the voices of his two sons arguing schoolboy injustice. "Would you pass the salad, dear?" his wife interrupted him—but then she would know, they would all know, that he'd been right in his foreboding. One way or the other, was there any possibility that he left unturned?

But Nemerov was mistaken, in the letter if not in the spirit; anticipation could not contain nature. He died not suddenly at all, but with the knowledge a month before, that he was as good as dead and that it didn't matter when. Let the newspapers write it, he said to himself with a tranquility he had not known since his passion first flowered, and he turned then to the stack of mystery stories on his hospital table.

❈ ❈ ❈ ❈ ❈ ❈ ❈

3. Had Bynder been less modest in his looks and pretensions, the public at large would have heard of him. As it was, only a small group of colleagues who followed him on his rounds at the Brooklyn Hospital and a number of patients in the middle-class apartment houses along Ocean Parkway knew him professionally, and they had no power to call him to brighter eminence. It was not, Bynder himself acknowledged, a matter of intelligence; he had only a conventional memory, and many other members of his class at medical school knew more than he did of physiology and the concepts of science. Perhaps, he told himself more than once, he was a painter misplaced. For what distinguished Bynder was an uncanny eye, a sense for the look of whatever it was he was seeing. He

first noticed this talent in the training hospital when he found himself quite exactly predicting what the professor would say about the patients around whom the group of students assembled. This ability had not seemed to him extraordinary; he assumed that the other students were doing the same thing. Only after the professor made a couple of obvious errors did Bynder realize that the other students had not noticed. He kept close track of the two patients, and when, in the one case, cardiac insufficiency revealed itself as ulcer and, in the other, nervous fatigue lost out to leukemia, Bynder acknowledged the intensity of a strange power.

After he went into practice for himself, he missed the facts on only a few occasions, and these he was able to explain in terms of his own state during the diagnosis. He knew that to be accurate, he had somehow to step outside both himself and the patient; when his eye took over his consciousness, the eye never failed. His colleagues at the hospital became aware of this ability, and Bynder was often called in by them for consultation.

His work was, pretty much, Bynder's life. He had married late and was childless. There were few outside interests or friends; if he had been asked to fill out a questionnaire that called for his hobbies, he would have put down only the one word, *Looking*.

As with most gifts, however, this one had its price. The patients he examined during office hours or on his rounds did not, it turned out, set the limits of his attention. Bynder's eye could not rest even when he stepped outside his office or the hospital; the game it played with him was one about which he never spoke, one which he had a difficult time admitting to himself. He would leave the office after a restless day of probing and looking, but his eye was indefatigable, ruled by a stern commitment. Walking to the subway, he would keep track of the people on the crowded rush-hour sidewalks. The people were unknown to him except by as much as they revealed in their faces and postures; rarely would he pass any of them twice. But he found himself, each time he isolated a figure, making a diagnosis—not only of the present, but of the future, the narrow future of death's manner: what it would be. It was a game that reminded him of children who would not step on the pavement lines; a short time of playing the game, and they played it even when they weren't looking. Only his game was looking.

In most of this, of course, Bynder would never know how accurate he was. But his work did not stop on the crowded sidewalks or in the subway. There was, for example, the building superintendent and his wife; the Sanders in 3A who were the only friends he and his wife had in their apartment house; the newspaper man, nameless, who from his kiosk sold Bynder a paper each weekday evening. They too, all of them, along with Bynder's family, were duly marked and noted. (His wife had only one cousin in California, whom he had never met. But they spoke on the phone, and Bynder heard in her voice the latency of heart disease). Bynder's eye, like that of a connoisseur turned loose in a museum where the title plates had been removed, never faltered. The superintendent had to leave when the tremors of Parkinson's disease could no longer be concealed; Mrs. Sander suddenly began to gasp and fade. How Bynder foresaw all this, he never knew himself. He had only to look at the person—a matter of posture or build, the set or coloring of the face, and the intuition came.

In a controlled and orderly life, there was one thing Bynder could not get himself to do (it began with the discovery of his power); that was to look in a mirror. He had even learned to shave by touch.

✿ ✿ ✿ ✿ ✿ ✿ ✿ ✿

And ½. We speak of the illusion of immortality—that unconscious present when careless health and a bright sun stare the future out of countenance. But isn't there an opposite illusion as well, of mortality? Imagine the life of a man so persuaded of his mortality, so incapable either of postponing it or of living with it in prospect, that he counted each minute as his end. Survival could give him no comfort, for each passing minute brought a new present. The expectation was always on him; even his friends would complain (more rightly than they knew) that his mind was always someplace else.

This man was long remembered by his doctor. "When I told him that he had only eight months to live," the doctor repeated to his colleagues many times and always with a sense of wonder, "he gave a great sigh of relief. This was, he said, the first time he had such solid assurance."